# THE SCOTCH WHISKY
# DRINKER'S COMPANION

*Also by* ALBERT D. MACKIE

POEMS IN TWO TONGUES

A CALL FROM WARSAW

SING A SANG O' SCOTLAND

EDINBURGH

THE BOOK OF MACNIB

THE HEARTS

GENTLE LIKE A DOVE

EDINBURGH: AN INDUSTRIAL HISTORY

A TALE OF TWO BRIDGES

SCOTTISH PAGEANTRY

DONALD'S DIVE

THE SCOTCH COMEDIANS

# THE SCOTCH WHISKY DRINKER'S COMPANION

ALBERT D. MACKIE

THE RAMSAY HEAD PRESS · EDINBURGH

First published in 1973 by
The Ramsay Head Press
36 Castle Street
Edinburgh EH2 3BN

Printed in Scotland by
Macdonald Printers (Edinburgh) Ltd.
Loanhead, Midlothian

# Acknowledgements

The author thanks the Scotch Whisky industry as a whole for assistance in his inquiries—in particular, the Scotch Whisky Association, the Distillers Company Ltd, John Haig & Co. Ltd, White Horse Distillers Ltd, John Crabbie & Co. Ltd, Arthur Bell & Sons Ltd, Charles Mackinlay & Co. Ltd, Long John International Ltd, the House of Fraser Ltd, and Dalmore, Whyte & Mackay Ltd, also the Drambuie Liqueur Co. Ltd.

Thanks to the following are due for permission to reproduce photographs: Distillers Company Ltd, Mackinlay McPherson Ltd, John Walker & Sons Ltd, and White Horse Distillers Ltd.

# Contents

# Illustrations

# 1    What is Scotch?

WE SCOTS claimed we came from the Middle East by a circuitous route to the country anciently known as Caledonia, which we now call Scotland. It is a country of rocky mountains and pure, swift-running rivers, of peaty uplands and fertile plains, of innumerable sea inlets and inland lakes, islands and woodlands. If some countries have a lot of sand, we have a lot of water. G. K. Chesterton sang: "I don't care where the water goes, if it doesn't get into the wine;" but in what we call "the wine of the country," water is all-important.

When we came here, and long after, until we started to read and write and so lost our long memories, we claimed to be descendants of Scota, the daughter of Pharaoh of Egypt. It was from her, we said, that we took our name. We claimed also to have journeyed from the Holy Land. On our way we lingered some time in Greece, and so our old poets referred to us as the Gael of Greece. We asserted that we brought with us all the way from Bethel the stone

11

which Jacob used as a pillow the time he had that famous dream. We called it the Stone of Destiny, or, in Gaelic, the Lia Fail. On this we crowned our kings, until King Edward I of England—called "the Hammer of the Scots" because he, by his determination to crush us, was the man who hammered us together as a nation—took our Stone to Westminster as a trophy.

We brought something else with us when we came to Caledonia, all that way from the Middle East and ancient Greece by way of Ireland, to our settlements in Argyll and thence into the Highlands. It was something which we shared with the Gaels we left behind us in Ireland—the art of making whisky.

This, anyway, is the tale as I tell it, as a Scot descended from those Gaels who came over from Ireland, but also with a touch in me of the Picts who were on Speyside before the Scots arrived, and almost certainly of those ancient Caledonians who were a stumbling block to the Romans in their attempt to colonise all Britain.

Much of what we were, before Agricola, or before the Venerable Bede, began putting what they could glean of us into written records, is necessarily lost, unless we accept those traditions to which we swore so long ago. In particular it is quite obscure when, how or where we began turning barley into whisky with the aid of pure water and peat. Agricola did not know about that, or his historian Tacitus. If they did know about Scotch whisky, like good soldiers and cunning travellers they kept quiet about it. Much later, the Venerable Bede, who noted the different peoples and languages there were in Scotland in his day, did not mention Scotch whisky either, but he also may have been a foxy chronicler. A lot of people knew about Scotch whisky without wanting to tell the world, for it was the sort of discovery that, in days of scarcity, one would naturally want to keep to oneself. Especially if one had any experience of the encroachments of the State, and of the civil servants who must always be meddling with anything which people want to enjoy.

It is quite far on in Scottish history before we start making much of a murmur about our precious product, but that is no indication whatever of how long we have been making the stuff. Even after officialdom from Edinburgh and London began to meddle in our Highland affairs and particularly to take notice of our whisky, a lot of us were engaged in keeping the whereabouts of our distilleries a secret, and in smuggling the good stuff out as circumspectly as possible, besides keeping as much as we could for our own imbibing.

We may well have learned to distil from the Egyptians or the Arabs long before we came to Scotland. When we came to Scotland we knew that a great spirit could be distilled from fermented barley, and we recognised Scotland as a place where good barley could be grown.

One of our islands—Tiree—is also known in Gaelic as Tir an Eorna, land of barley. This crop, along with oats, was best suited to cultivation in many parts of the islands and mainlands which the Scots gradually populated. Porridge made from oatmeal became our staple diet. Whisky made from barley became our national drink. And the barley also fed our cattle, which were to become famous for milk and beef.

Even if whisky goes back to the days when the Scots were colonising Caledonia, or at latest to the missionary centuries of the Gaelic monks—the sixth and seventh centuries—there is still no certain historical reference to the spirit before the fifteenth century, when the use of malt in the making of aquavitae is mentioned. But it seems from the reference to have been a well established undertaking by that time. The first distillery actually to be mentioned by name in official records occurs as late as the seventeenth century. It is Ferintosh in the Black Isle district of Ross and Cromarty, owned by Duncan Forbes of Culloden, to which reference is made in the Acts of the Scottish Parliament in the year 1699. But there are early references to the making of aquavitae in Banffshire, and to the use of the spirit at funerals, a grand old Highland custom.

*Aquavitae* it is called in old Scottish records. The literal translation into Gaelic is *uisge beatha,* pronounced in modern Gaelic *ooshka bay-ha*—the water of life. This is the origin of the word *whisky* (in Scotland we spell it without the *e,* though there is no historical or philological reason for any of the spellings—only, when you look at a Scotch whisky label, see that it is spelt *whisky*).

To us, more than to the brandy-makers who used the word *aquavitae,* the word for water stood for virtue and purity. There is no water in the world to surpass, and there are few waters to equal, the water that runs down the mountainsides of Scotland— the streams, the springs, the wells, the lakes. The melted snow which cascades over our clean, hard rocks and seeps through our clean and fragrant mosses. *Uisge*, water, became the operative word. *Beatha*, of life, went without saying.

The only further specification it required, as an everlasting guarantee of the honesty and integrity with which it was made, was the word *Scotch*. So today you do not simply ask for *whisky*. Above all you ask for *Scotch*. That word means strength and purity. The great Gaelic virtues were hardiness, heroism and pride—not vanity but a constant consciousness of the need to keep up one's good name. The French who knew us as soldiers, in their *Garde Ecossaise*, had a phrase, *Fier comme un Ecossais*—as proud as a Scot. It is this constant consciousness of the need to keep up one's good name that is the guarantee that Scotch whisky means good whisky. It is the reason why we do not sell it until it is properly matured, and why, at every stage in its production, Scotch whisky is made with skill and integrity.

We Scots esteemed our hereditary art so highly that wherever we could grow barley, and the water and the air were good and pure, we made whisky. In the Highlands and the islands, and the uplands which break up our rather loosely-termed Lowlands, we have another asset which has become inseparable from the distilling of whisky—peat. Not only was it discovered to be valuable as the handiest fuel in the Highlands and Islands. It was discovered also to impart some of the imponderable virtues to the whisky. Its fragrance is distilled into the bouquet of our malt whiskies, and is preserved in varying degrees in the blends.

At one time in the Highlands almost every little grower of barley, with good water and aromatically combustible peat conveniently at hand, had his own little pot-still in a cave or in the heather, or built into his cottage, and made his own whisky—partly to pay the rent, partly to enjoy to himself. Until the people without culture—without, as we Scots say, the root of the matter in them—who came by stealth to make themselves rulers of the land, started to interfere, and to burden our valuable ancient customs with alien laws, at which our bards cried out in protest. For just as surely as barley made whisky, whisky made many of us poets.

Our greatest bard, Robert Burns, sang:

"Freedom and whisky gang thegither—
Tak aff your dram!"

Freedom and whisky go hand in hand, so quaff your glass. Burns may have meant to remind us at the same time that interference with freedom and interference with Scotch whisky came hand in hand, and from the same source.

If it is true, as our Gaelic tradition stoutly maintained, that we came from Egypt, the Holy Land and the Isles of Greece; that we had given up in our time the fleshpots of Egypt and a land flowing with milk and honey and those islands where grapes could be grown as they could not be grown in Caledonia, and that we had, by choice or compulsion, ventured into this rocky land which seems austere and barren by comparison with all three—perhaps, after all, we knew where we were going.

"Blessed are the meek, for they shall inherit the earth." Someone has pointed out that "meek" (*mic* in Gaelic spelling) is the plural of *Mac*.

Who knows but one of our pioneering adventurers—of whom we Scots have always had plenty—had nosed this land out; or perhaps it was a Phoenician trader who had been here and was able to tell us, that here was a land capable of yielding rich crops of barley, and that the water was the best in the world for distilling.

We Scots know a lot about water. Much of our realm is water. We live in it. It is our element. Some of our clans, such as the MacFarlanes of Loch Sloy, chose to live in the wettest parts of all Britain. We are supposed to be a thrifty race, cunning in the turning of simple things to profit. We have proved this in the use we have made of the one thing we had plenty of—water.

> So came *uisge beatha*, or as Burns spelt it *usquebae*—
> "Wi' tippenny, we fear nae evil, (tippenny=ale)
> Wi' usquebae, we'll face the Devil!"

Gaelic poets refer to it as *uisge beatha feadanach* or *uisge beatha nam feadan*, aquavitae of the pipes, referring to the pipe or worm through which the Highland malt whisky is distilled. English travellers heard it first as *usky*. Some of them heard it called, as they spelt it, *trestarig*. This meant thrice-distilled whisky. They picked up references also to a more potent variety called *usky baul*. This, they understood, was whisky four times distilled. So strong, it was said to be, that more than two spoonfuls of it "would stop a man's breath." It sounds like what the Americans call "Bullfrog Whiskey—Drink a little, hop a little, then croak."

15

In Gaelic, *treas tarruing*, pronounced *tress tarrik* by some Gaels, means "a third drawing, or distillation," and the term was used to describe good whisky, although two distillations are sufficient to make the best whisky of today. *Uisge beatha ball*, in Gaelic, would mean "spot whisky"—the acme of perfection—but if it was indeed capable of stopping a man's breath it obviously needed breaking down—that is to say, reduced in strength by dilution with pure water. It is surely no purpose of drinking good whisky, to stop one's breath.

The garnering of barley seed for the further sowing of barley is mentioned in St Adamnan's life of St Columba (sixth century), Barley and oats were sown by the first Scots to settle in Caledonia. both for the feeding of their cattle and for food for themselves. A certain amount was kept for brewing and probably for distilling. The threshing of oats and barley was by flail. There is reference thus early to a kiln in Iona for the drying of grain, and such a kiln could be used in distilling. Bronze vessels were available from early times. Technologically there was nothing to prevent distilling from the time the first Scots settled in Argyll.

*Treas tarruing* is mentioned several times in Gaelic poetry and prose of the sixteenth and later centuries. In 1596 "ane gallon of sufficient aquavite" formed part of the reddendo for lands in Ardchattan, a reference to home-distilled whisky as a fair and possible means of payment.

Mary MacLeod, the seventeenth century Skye poetess, refers to *treas tarruing* in her poem on MacLeod's wedding:

"To me was known MacLeod's custom, broaching wine, drinking beer and filling the stoup with the thrice-distilled stuff, the necessary spur to promote enjoyment."

Mary died in 1705 with the praise of whisky on her lips:

"Ho ro, how I enjoy the dram!
Many a person is indebted to it."

It had helped to keep her alive till the age of 105.

Her praise of the beverage was echoed in Gaelic, Scots and English by many of our poets who followed her. A somewhat later Gaelic bard, Duncan Ban Macintyre, who was a soldier in Edinburgh's old Town Guard in the eighteenth century, was brought up before the city magistrates and charged with the manufacture and sale of illicitly distilled whisky. His wife Mary

The Speyside distillery of Cardow, Knockando, has been making whisky since 1824 Used in the famous Johnnie Walker blend the whisky is also available as a twelve-year-old single called Cardhu Highland Malt.

*Left*
The stillroom at the Cardow distillery contains six copper pot stills. Three are "wash stills" in which the first distillation takes place, and three are "spirit stills" where the spirit is finally distilled.

*Below*
In the maltings of the Balmenach Distillery, Cromdale, the temperature of the germinating barley is noted, and controlled by varying the circulation of air.

(Mairi Bhan Og) was celebrated as an expert distiller with a pot-still concealed somewhere behind her popular "howff" or pub in the Royal Mile—in the Lawnmarket part of that stretch from the Castle to Holyrood Palace. No doubt some of the magistrates had been among her customers. Duncan's answer to the charge was that he had drunk more whisky than he had ever made. The case against him was dismissed.

Duncan's *Song of the Bottle* declares:

"The elegant stuff will cause us to sing in melody.
Its joy will make our conversation more eloquent.
This is the true sweet drink which assuages our thirst.
Sad would we be if it were taken from us.
A health to the heroes, the splendid Highlanders,
Whose custom it was to drink down their dram!
They were ever lovers of the tasty stuff."

He liked his whisky, he tells us, in a silver goblet—a hint to modern whisky drinkers from an eighteenth century expert.

In the eighteenth century half a million gallons of whisky was being produced in Scotland and already by the 1780s there was a substantial export to England. Much of it was smuggled from secret stills in the Highlands, carried through the mountain passes by the farmers using the rough and sturdy little Highland ponies, known as "garrons," laden with casks. These secret distillers and smugglers were the founders of the Scotch whisky trade. There are many amusing stories about whisky smuggling still told in the Highlands. An Edinburgh city officer called Archie Campbell, whose people were Highland, decided to bury his mother in the family burial ground in the North when she died in the Scottish capital. He hired a hearse to carry her to the Highlands, and came back with it full of illicit whisky. He told his friends in extenuation: "I took away the mortal remains, but brought back the spirit."

When King George IV, on his State visit to Edinburgh in 1822, demanded Glenlivet whisky and would accept no spurious substitute, he knew full well it must come to him from a source not yet hallowed by law.

But just as we had to change the word *uisge beatha* to *whisky* to make it easier for Anglo-Saxons to pronounce, the history of the elixir from the eighteenth century onwards has been one of accommodation of the trade to the English and others whose tastes were somewhat different from those of the old Highlanders. It is not the pure malt whiskies of the North that have conquered the world, so much as the relatively modern proprietary brands which effect a compromise with world-wide and modern taste, though they are still based on the malts and still good Scotch whisky, through and through, made with the same care at every stage as the products of the famous Highland pot-stills.

So if I claim that the best whisky is the original Highland malt made in the old-fashioned pot-still, it must be understood that I am writing as a bigoted Scot. There are people in the Highlands—and especially dwelling around the distillery-rich regions of Speyside, Lossieside, Findhorn and Forres, with the smell of peat smoke in their nostrils, who drink nothing but the pure Highland malt whisky of their own localities. On the other hand, we are a hospitable race, and we are broadminded enough to appreciate that it is not everyone who will prefer The Glenlivet, Glenfiddich or any other of the ancient, celebrated and delectable malts. "Everybody to their own taste, as the old wife said when she kissed the cow"—is an old Highland proverb. There are indeed some charming blends of Highland or Lowland malt whiskies with whisky distilled from grain by means of the patent still, which will appeal to palates, and soothe stomachs, all around the world, and which are still, as I have said, thoroughly Scotch.

So what is Scotch? It is a Highland malt, an Islay malt, a Campbeltown (Kintyre) malt or a Lowland malt, or it is a blend of several of these with grain whisky, distilled, casked and matured in Scotland. That is the gist of the legal definition and the requirements of honest trade description.

All Scotch whisky has in it the virtues of the original malts, but the blends add the qualities of the grain whiskies, which are lighter but are also made from the best Scottish water and Scotch-distilled and matured. A Royal Commission in 1909 concluded: "Blending for the English and foreign markets on a large scale seems to have commenced between thirty and forty years ago. Since that time the practice has gone on increasingly. It has undoubtedly done very much to popularise Scotch whisky. The market for blended whiskies is greater than for individual whiskies: so much so that it would probably be safe to say that the majority of Englishmen who drink whisky seldom drink anything but a blend."

It might be said likewise of the majority of Scots, who are not by any means all Speyside Fundamentalists. The general conclusion of the Commission was that whisky was "a spirit obtained by distillation of a mash of cereal grains saccharified by the diastase of malt," and that Scotch whisky was whisky, as thus defined, distilled in Scotland.

In fact Scotch whisky is largely manufactured by means of the old pot-still, almost unmodified. The growth of the demand for th product has necessitated advances in manufacturing methods and the introduction of labour-saving plant. But the malt whiskies— whether made north of the Highland Line (an imaginary boundary drawn across Scotland from Dundee to Greenock) or on the island of Islay, or in the peninsula of Kintyre at Campbeltown, or here and there throughout the Lowlands—is made exclusively from malted barley in pot-stills of ancient type.

It is made only in the cool months of the year and in the pure air of our countryside, often high in the hills or near the sea. The water from which it is made is drawn from the purest sources of mountain stream and spring. A peat fire is used in its manufacture, and the fragrance of the peat gives the whisky part of its friendly bouquet and other indefinable virtues. Only the best barley is used, much of it grown in the surrounding countryside and within easy reach of the distillery, in regions where it has been grown for this purpose for centuries, supplemented by imports—again only of the best and most suitable for the making of whisky. Added to all these preconditions are the experience, skill and thorough training and integrity of generations of born distillers.

Grain whisky is made in the Coffey Still patented about a hundred years ago. Here also malted barley is used, but along with maize and other cereals, producing a lighter and less strongly flavoured but none the less true Scotch spirit. Both grain and malt whiskies are matured for years in oak casks to produce a spirit of smoothness, mellowness and purity. Furthermore, when malts and grain spirits are blended together after maturing, their blend is returned to cask and left for months, as they say, to "marry," before being bottled and packed for distribution and sale at home or overseas. The essential quality of the product comes from care at every stage of manufacture.

The process of continuous distillation which speeded up the production of Scotch—particularly in the Lowlands—was pioneered in 1826 by Robert Stein of Kincardine, but the technique was perfected by Aeneas Coffey of Dublin. Coffey's Patent Still, introduced into the Lowlands of Scotland, made possible the production of a bland grain spirit, more economical than the output of the pot-stills.

As might be expected from such technological change, it led to a complete revolution in the structure of the whisky trade, and eventually to combinations of distillers, mergers and take-overs. Conspicuously it led to the formation in 1877 of the Distillers Company Limited, which in its turn led to further development in the restructuring of the industry and in the blending and marketing of whisky.

From the Highland pot-stills of the fifteenth and earlier centuries to the highly organised and automated distillery, blending and bottling plant of today is a long and interesting story. Local conditions determined the siting of the most durable and successful stills; individual talents and enterprise gave the developments their particular bias here and there; wars and politics affected growth, stopping it here, boosting it there.

The lofty mountains of the Cairngorm (Blue Peak) and Monadhliath (Grey Moor) ranges, with their fast streams and crystal springs, were the backbone of Highland whisky-making. Upland peat mosses filtered the water and provided the fuel for the drying of the malted barley and the fragrance and full-bodied taste which the whisky drinker loves, and which are present in the most refined blends. The broad rolling fertile plains, of the North-East and Moray Firth area in particular, provided the barley.

The zigzag Scottish coast line, as well as the sequestered mountain passes, furnished discreet routes for the products of the old illicit stills and helped to establish those Highland fastnesses and coastal villages as ideal for the trade, and coppersmiths arose in Banffshire skilled in making pot stills for the secret manufacture of the elixir, which became a cherished export to England about the beginning of the nineteenth century, while its manufacture was still illegal.

Thus we find Sir Walter Scott in 1813 writing from Edinburgh to Joanna Bailie in Hampstead: "I am very glad that the whisky came safe: do not stint so laudable an admiration for the liquor of Caledonia, for I have plenty of right good and sound Highland Ferintosh, and I can always find an opportunity of sending you up a bottle."

The distiller's enemy was the tax-gatherer, backed by the power of the alien sword. The Scots Parliament in 1644 passed an Excise Act. The duty was 2s 8d per pint of aqua vitae or other strong liquor. English interference began soon after the Treaty of Union of 1707, which combined the Parliaments of the two countries. The long arm of the revenue department came across the Border and stretched up into the Highlands, probing at the private distilling which had become part of the Gaelic way of life. And the tax kept rising. The only way it ever goes is up. In 1714 came the malt tax to challenge the foxiest guile of the north-country secret distillers and smugglers.

In 1784 the Highlanders considered themselves singled out and victimised by the Wash Act which imposed a different tax system on them from that suffered by the Lowlanders. While the tax in the South was levied on the basis of a hundred gallons of wash with an estimated yield of twenty gallons of spirit of one to ten overproof, in the Highlands there was a licence duty on stills at a rate of twenty shillings a gallon of still content. The minimum capacity of a still was limited at twenty gallons. Next the Highland distilleries were limited to a production of 250 bolls of malt free of duty and 1660 gallons of spirit for a still of forty gallons, with the minimum capacity fixed at thirty gallons. Furthermore, the spirits produced in the Highlands must not be moved out of the region.

Highlanders have never been famous for respecting laws which were not of their own wish or making. The 1785 ban on the transport of their whisky beyond their bounds led to wholesale smuggling centred in Speyside, particularly in Glenlivet, which had already won the affection of discerning drinkers in the South.

When, following upon a Royal Commission, the 1823 Act made it possible for the Highland distillers to license their stills of upwards of forty gallons at a fee of £10 and sell their whisky outside of the region, with the tax at 2s 3d a gallon of proof spirit, a farmer at Glenlivet, named George Smith, was the first to take advantage of the new situation, apply for a licence and establish the pioneer legalised distillery. His step into the legitimate trade at first aroused the enmity of those who had built up a thriving business in the illicit manufacture and transport of whisky. He had to carry arms to protect himself and establish his business in an atmosphere of threats of violence.

Taxation continued to rise. By 1840 the duty was 5d a bottle.

It was the contention of the malt distillers, that theirs—produced from malted barley by a special process of distillation and matured to give a recognised flavour and quality—was the only true claimant to the title *Scotch*, that led to the whisky definition proceedings of 1905.

The Royal Commission's findings established that the products of the grain distilleries, and their blends with malt, could legitimately be called *Scotch*.

From then on, the trade, stimulated by the introduction of more modern methods of manufacture, packaging and marketing, grew to world dimensions. The two world wars, with their need to conserve food supplies, and the period of Prohibition in the United States, involved temporary interruptions in the story of progress, and taxation had its effect on home consumption. Before the first World War a bottle of good old Scotch whisky could be bought for half a crown (now represented by 12½p). Later it went on to cost from 3s (15p) to 4s 6d (22½p). After the war, Will Fyffe was singing a mournful ditty about "the price of food" as "twelve and a tanner a bottle." That would be 62½ new pence, which we should hardly consider now to be a lot to pay for a bottle of the Real McKay.

The duty on a bottle of whisky at the start of the first World War was 1s 8½d (more than 8½p). By 1939 it was 9s 7½d (more than 48p) and the bottle cost the consumer 14s 3d (71½p). Now the duty per bottle is £2.20 (£18.85 per proof gallon, compared with £9.54 in 1947). The cost of a bottle to the purchaser at a United Kingdom bar or wineshop represents taxation to the extent of 75 to 85 per cent. Between 30 and 75p of the price of the bottle at £2.50 to £2.95 goes to the making and long storage of the whisky, its carriage, sales promotion, distribution, selling, administration expenses and profits for the wholesaler and retailer. Every drop which the Scotch whisky drinker at home sips represents a substantial hand-out to the Government, so the imbiber of Scotch in the United Kingdom is standing in the front line of patriotic duty.

The Prohibition era meant the closing, except for loopholes open again to the smugglers, of what has since become Scotland's biggest export market—the United States.

At the beginning of the first World War the export of Scotch had been 10 million proof gallons. In 1918–19 it was down to 2.79 million gallons. Stocks were gradually built up (Scotch has to be at least three years old, that is three years maturing in bond, before its release for sale) and by 1924–5 we were exporting 8.23 million proof gallons.

With the repeal of Prohibition in the United States in 1933, about a hundred Scotch distilleries were restored to life, and began to build up their stocks for the new trade.

In the middle of the Second World War (1942) the Scotch Whisky Association was formed to protect and promote the interests of the trade. Whisky helped to pay for the sinews of war. It was rationed on the home market, and once again Scotch whisky drinkers suffered for their country.

After the war the export trade mounted steadily from 4.7 million proof gallons in 1945 to 70,327,775 in 1971.

# 2 The Art of the Distiller

THE BARLEY for Highland and other malt whiskies may be of neighbourhood growth, as it was in the early days of the industry, or it may be imported, or a mixture of both. The essential thing is that it has to be right for malting. Extreme care is taken in its choice and storage.

It has to be the product of a good harvest and in good colour and condition. Denmark, Australia and California are three reliable sources of good whisky-making barley to augment the home harvest.

From the barley selected for the process, any unwanted ingredients are removed by screening. The barley is then put into water-tanks, or "steeps," as they are called. In these it soaks for two or three days. When the moisture has penetrated right into each grain, the barley is spread out on the malting floor, thickly, in order to generate heat and start the germinating process. The malting floor is of concrete. The germination takes from eight to twelve days, according to the season, the type of barley and other factors.

All through this process, the maltman keeps turning the barley at intervals. This regulates the temperature and the rate of germination. The hotter the weather, the more often the barley is turned. In the course of the germination, the barley secretes enzyme diastase. This renders the starch soluble and facilitates its conversion into sugar.

When the barley has reached the stage when it is known as "green malt," it is dried in a kiln. This stops the germination at the right stage. The kiln floor is pitted with innumerable holes. A fire under that, burning a mixture of coke and peat, flavours and dries the malt. It is the "peat reek" passing through the malt in the drying process that gives the whisky its Highland—and indeed its particular local—accent. The peat usually comes from the neighbourhood, or may be brought in from other parts of the countryside, mostly Highlands and Hebridean islands. Its fragrant aroma is part of the characteristic atmosphere of a distillery district. You smell it whenever you step into Keith or Dufftown, for instance, and it means that whisky is a-making.

Under modern conditions, the malting may be carried out under mechanical control in Saladin boxes or in drum maltings. Some distilleries obtain their malt from centralised maltings under the more organised conditions of today.

When the malt has been dried in the kiln it is put into a mill which grinds it into grist, after a short rest in the malt loft and another screening, to remove dried rootlets which may occur. The grist is mixed with hot water and the mixture runs into the big mash tun. It is in this that the conversion occurs from starch to sugar. The soluble starch is converted into a sugary liquid called "wort." This is drawn off, leaving in the mash tun a solid matter known as "draff." This is a by-product of whisky-making which has proved to be a valuable feeding stuff for cattle. The Highland pot-stills are situated for the most part in cattle country, so the process contributes vastly to another staple Scottish industry.

The malting and mashing stages have been completed. The cooled "wort" passes into large containers called "wash backs." These have a capacity of anything from two to ten thousand gallons.

27

Yeast is added. The live yeast attacks the sugar and converts it into crude alcohol in a fermented liquid called "wash." After about forty-eight hours of fermentation the "wash"—including alcohol along with unfermented matter and some by-products—has reached the stage of distillation.

It goes into large copper pot-stills. These are heated to turn the alcohol into vapour. The vapour rises up the still and goes into the cooling plant. This is the traditional coiled copper tube known as the "worm." This tube is kept in continually running water. There are other types of condenser in use. But whatever the device, the function of the cooling plant is to condense the alcoholic vapour into liquid form.

As I stated in the first chapter, despite the legend of *trestarig* (the third distillation), the malt whisky is only twice distilled. The first distillation separates the alcohol from the fermented liquid. It also eliminates what has been left of the yeast and the unfermentable matter. The resultant clear liquid is called "low wines." It passes through the sampling safe to the low wines charger.

From this container the distillate is pumped into the low wines still. In this it goes through the second distillation. Once more from this it passes through the sampling safe.

The first runnings, or "foreshot," are not considered drinkable. The "middle run" is carefully checked. If it meets the distiller's standard of quality it is accepted as "spirit" and flows into the spirit receiver. At the first sign of deterioration in strength or quality, the run is diverted. The beginning, and the end of the run, called "feints," are drawn off to be redistilled in the low wines still with the next distillate from the wash still.

Highland distilleries usually distil up to the warm months, when conditions are not so suitable for good whisky-making. Holidays and other arrangements can be worked into this otherwise quiescent period.

From the spirit-receiver, the whisky which has been collected goes to be diluted with water to the correct strength for maturing. This takes place in oak casks, left lying in bonded warehouses for a minimum period of five years. The nature of the casks allows air to permeate the spirit and create the process of maturing and mellowing.

In contrast to the intermittent method of distillation in pot stills, grain whisky is made by a continuous process in the patent still. Its mash is not of malted barley alone but contains also unmalted cereals. The proportions of barley to other cereals vary from distillery to distillery.

The unmalted cereals, after being ground, are cooked under steam pressure. This process, lasting about three and a half hours, in converters, with the mixture of grain and water stirred automatically throughout, causes the grain to gelatinize or burst its starch cells.

The resultant liquid now joins the malted barley in the mash tun. Here the diastase in the malted barley turns the starch into sugar or maltose. As in the manufacture of malt whisky, the biochemical changes in the course of fermentation produce spirit, along with carbon dioxide.

Wort is collected at a lower specific gravity than in the pot stills. Paradoxically, on distillation in the Coffey Still, the spirit is collected at a much higher strength.

In the making of the malt whiskies, distillation occupies two separate stages. It is interrupted, also, when the stills are emptied and refilled. In contrast to this, the making of grain whisky is a continuous process, in a quite different type of apparatus.

There are two forty or fifty feet tall columns in the Coffey Patent Still. They are of copper, joined by piping, closed and rectangular in section. Inside, they are divided into several storeys of chambers, separated by perforated plates, laid horizontally.

One column is the analyser and the other is the rectifier.

Steam is fed into the foot of the analyser. Hot wash is led in at the top. They meet on the surface of the perforated plates. There the wash boils.

Alcoholic vapour mixed with uncondensed steam, like the low wines of the malt whisky process, climbs to the top of the analyser column. The spent wash runs down the other way and is led off from the foot.

Out of the top of the analyser column, the hot vapours proceed by the vapour pipe into the foot of the rectifier column, to rise through the chambers and condense to some extent on the sections of a long coil through which cold wash is flowing. At the same time the wash as it progresses through the coil is being heated by the action of the hot vapour, and it proceeds hot into the top of the analyser to maintain the continuous process.

The rectifier progressively cools down the crude alcohol mixture and separates out the spirit which is fit to drink. The partial condensation on the coil on its way up inside the rectifier leaves a practically pure spirit vapour to reach the top. There it condenses on a water frame which is cooled separately. From there it is run off to the spirit safe through a cooling worm. Thus it makes its way to the spirit receiver.

Volatile residues, somewhat like the foreshots of the pot still process, pass through a vapour vent at the top of the rectifier column. The hot feints, which contain the less volatile liquids and some of the spirit, are fed back to the top of the analyser—the wash and feints inlet trough, to circulate again through the still. So the merry-go-round continues. The spirit, to parody the song, goes round and around . . . and it comes out here.

It is all done under strict supervision by the stillman, who occupies a working platform near the top of the rectifier, where he can observe and keep under control the temperatures, gravities and rates of flow of the wash, the spirit, the low wines, vapours and other liquids as they circulate between and through the columns. As in the case of the malt stills, there are tests all the time at the spirit safe. In this way the quality is regulated, and consistency is maintained.

Whether the whisky is pure malt or grain, it has to be matured. After distillation it is run into oak casks.

Spirit as it comes from the still at first has no colour. It is quite drinkable, but it tastes rough and tends to parch the palate rather than quench the thirst. It takes years of maturation in the oak cask to make it smooth and mellow to drink. The permeable oak wood permits air to seep in. Evaporation takes place, improving the spirit and mellowing it. Grain whisky, being less highly flavoured, takes less time to mature. Malt may be kept as long as fifteen years, or even more, in the oak cask. There are various factors affecting the timing of maturation. Size of casks, strength of the spirit at the storing stage and conditions in the particular warehouse, including humidity of the atmosphere, and temperature, all play their part.

The minimum age for whisky before consumption is three years. Some overseas nations importing Scotch may demand up to five years' maturation before accepting it.

Malt whiskies are matured for seven, ten or twelve years or longer. The drinker should always remember that if an age is quoted on the brand or vatted malt label, it is the age of the *youngest* whisky in the blend, which may contain others much older.

Once it has left the cask or vat and gone into the bottle, the whisky does not mature further. In fact, if it is good, it won't live much longer at the hands of the whisky drinker and his friends, of whom he is sure to have many.

But if you choose to keep it a long time, you can be sure it will not deteriorate, and even when it is opened there is no danger of its turning into anything else, like the wines which become vinegar.

Scotch whisky, furthermore, may be served in most room temperatures. Icing, keeping in a fridge, or serving with ice, are all a matter of choice.

Scotch as distilled consists of ethyl alcohol and water—again good Scotch water—and other constituents believed to represent essential oils from the cereals, and some derivatives from the peat used to dry the malt in the kilns.

Because of the different process by which it is produced, grain whisky features considerably less of these other constituents than malt whisky. It is a lighter spirit. It is less strongly flavoured, less aromatic.

Certainly the various malt whiskies are noted for their distinctive peaty and smoky bouquets. They are redolent of the countryside in which they are made.

Whisky made in different districts has different flavours and aromas. These are conditioned by the nature of the local water, peat and climate, which can be very local indeed in Scotland.

Distillers make it their business to keep their own whiskies consistent in character. Therein lies their skill—indeed, it is an arcane art. It comes only from ages of experience and training and the local transmission of tradition from one distilling generation to another. The art of the blender, with which I deal in Chapter Five, is all important also in determining the character of a proprietary brand, which again has to be consistent in every respect, so that the customer, when he orders a "Standfast," a Bell's, a Haig or a Crawford's, knows exactly what to expect, and if he knows his whisky, he cannot be fooled, even when it is served in a glass with the labelled bottle out of sight.

That is if he really knows his whisky. He would be a marvellous man who could tell all the singles and all the two thousand brands.

31

There is a Highland story of the man who swore he could tell any whisky blindfold.

With his eyes covered, sure enough, he tasted and correctly named whisky after whisky. Then one wicked member of the company whispered: "Try him with water!"

The champion tasted and hesitated, tasted again and sighed. "Ah, you're beat!" they cried.

"No, no," he protested, "wait a bit! I think I remember this. I tasted it once when I was a laddie."

# 3 The Malt Distilleries

IN THE middle of the Volstead era, when Prohibition officially excluded whisky from the tables of United States citizens on their own soil, a member of that great nation was on holiday in the North of Scotland.

He was being shown around by a Highlander, who grew rather tired of the American's comparisons of the heights of Scottish mountains with the stupendous dimensions of the Rockies, the Yosemite Valley, the Grand Canyon and all the other wonders of the New World. The Scot took the American to a shoulder of Ben Rinnes, a mountain in Banffshire, and pointed north towards Dufftown.

"There's something," he said, "you won't see in your own country."

"What's that?" asked the American.

"Distilleries," answered the Scot, "and they're all *working*."

33

Now there are flaws in this good old story. First of all, it was not true that there were no distilleries working then in America, but that is another story. Nor was it true that the Volstead enactment left the Scotch distilleries unaffected.

But it was true that there was—as there is today—a grand cluster of distilleries in that part of Scotland, just south of the Moray Firth and within easy travelling distance of Balmoral. As John Brown said to Queen Victoria: "A grand sicht, Mem!"

There are Islay malt distilleries, Campbeltown malt distilleries and even Lowland malt distilleries, and these will all be dealt with later in this chapter, but most romantic in their appeal to Scotch whisky drinkers are the Highland malt distilleries which have evolved from the private stills of the North Country crofters and farmers of long ago. Only a few of their products are available for drinking as single whiskies: these are discussed later. Mostly the products of the malt distilleries go to the blenders to join the grain whisky in creating the highly individual brands, blended and bottled largely in the Lowlands.

The majority of the Highland malt distilleries are on Speyside, around the burghs of Elgin, Rothes, Craigellachie, Keith and Dufftown—in Morayshire and Banffshire. Most celebrated is Glenlivet, whose popularity last century gave rise to the practice of referring to other distilleries in the neighbourhood as "Glenlivet," much as one would say *champagne*. Later, by legal agreement, it was laid down that the description should be joined by hyphen to the particular name of each distillery claiming this description, and the original Glenlivet distillery, and its single whisky, are both now designated "*The* Glenlivet."

Here are the Highland malt distilleries arranged in alphabetical order with some details of their situation, history and ownership:

ABERFELDY, Perthshire. The name comes from *Obar-Pheallaidh*, confluence of Peallaidh, this being an old Gaelic name of a water spirit. Last century, Grandtully Distillery, Aberfeldy, was noted as the smallest in the land and renowned for its pure Highland malt produced at a rate of 5,000 gallons a year. Aberfeldy Distillery of today, built in 1896, produces good Perthshire malt whisky and is owned by John Dewar & Sons Ltd., one of the companies which pioneered in the world marketing of Scotch and

A screw conveyor moving barley towards the steeping tank at the Linkwood Distillery, Elgin.

A mixture of malt grist and hot water enters the mash-tun. The mixture ("wort") is then fermented by the addition of yeast (Aberfeldy Distillery, Perthshire).

At the Talisker Distillery in the Isle of Skye a still-man prepares to empty a pot still at the end of a distillation by opening the air-cran.

which led also in the formation of The Distillers Company Ltd. (DCL). I shall indicate DCL distillers hereafter, as well as giving the names of the subsidiary companies operating the distilleries.

ABERLOUR-GLENLIVET, one of the Speyside distilleries, in Banffshire near Dufftown, a great malt whisky centre. Aberlour is a village at the foot of the 2,765 ft Benn Rinnes and on the Lour (*Labhair*, the chattering burn), a tributary of the fast-flowing great river Spey. The distillery was built in the 1860s and extended in 1880. Aberlour-Glenlivet Distillery Co. Ltd.

ARDMORE, Kennethmont, Aberdeenshire, built in 1891 by William Teacher. This is the original base of "Highland Cream" Scotch whisky. Wm. Teacher & Sons Ltd.

AUCHROISK (*achadh rùisg*, field of the fleece), Mulben. International Distillers and Vintners Ltd.

AULTMORE (great stream), Keith, Banffshire. Founded 1878 with a weekly output of 5,500 gallons. Fed by grand springs and fuelled at the drying kiln by peat from Forgie Moss. It produces a typical Speyside spirit. John and Robert Harvey & Co. Ltd. (DCL).

BALBLAIR (township of the battlefield), Edderton, Ross-shire. A quarter of a mile from Dornoch Firth. Founded in 1790, making it quite old, it was enlarged by Andrew Ross & Son in 1872. Edderton is called "The Parish of Peats" and has a wealth of streams considered highly suitable for distilling. Its whisky was renowned in the Glasgow, Leith and Aberdeen markets last century. Balblair Distillery Co. Ltd.

BALMENACH (the middle township), Cromdale, Morayshire. Ancestral distillery of the late Sir Robert Bruce Lockhart, who praised its product in his *Scotch* (Putnam, 1951). Innumerable hill streams of pure water, and the rugged, hidey-hole nature of the country made Cromdale a favourite with secret distillers and smugglers. Balmenach was one of the first of the licensed malt distilleries in the Highlands. James McGregor in 1824 brought his knowledge of distilling from Tomintoul, the highest village in the Highlands, and secured his licence the year after the Act of 1823. Balmenach 1873 whisky, said to be finer than old brandy, was supplied to Gairloch Hotel, Lochmaree, Wester Ross, in 1878 for the entertainment of Queen Victoria. Fine peat dug in the Burnside Moss at the foot of Cromdale Hill helped to give it its distinctive flavour. It became a well-known whisky around the British Empire last century. In 1887 John McGregor was proprietor and a limited liability company was formed in 1897 with the McGregors retaining control. John Crabbie & Co. Ltd. (DCL).

BALVENIE, Dufftown, Banffshire, built in 1890 by William Grant, clerk with Mortlach Distillery, who earlier built Glenfiddich. William Grant & Sons Ltd.

BANFF, on the Moray Firth coast, dates back to 1824. The name, by the way, comes from Banbha, an affectionate name for Ireland in Gaelic. The Scots, who came from Ireland, probably bringing with them the secret of whisky making, lovingly attached names for Ireland to many of their settlements, including this one. This distillery started at Mill of Banff, a mile from the town, then was rebuilt on a new site and rebuilt again after a fire in 1877. It was bombed in the Second World War. Slater, Rodger & Co. Ltd. (DCL).

BEN NEVIS, Fort William, at the foot of the highest mountain in Britain—Ben Nevis, 4,406 ft. Donald P. McDonald built the pier on the property of the Ben Nevis Distilleries. This was the first legal distillery in the Lochaber district. Most Scotch whisky drinkers are familiar with the nickname of the man who built it in 1825—Long John McDonald. In 1884–5 it produced 152,798 gallons of Long John's Dew of Ben Nevis. Ben Nevis Distillery (Fort William) Ltd.

BEN RIACH-GLENLIVET, Elgin. The Longmorn-Glenlivet Distilleries Ltd.

BENRINNES, Aberlour, Banffshire. Built in 1836, 1030 ft above sea-level on a site selected for the sake of the water rising from springs on the summit of the mountain. A. & A. Crawford Ltd. (DCL).

BENROMACH, Forres. One of the Forres-Findhorn group of distilleries built late last century. J. & W. Hardie Ltd. (DCL).

BEN WYVIS, Invergordon, Cromarty Firth, near Strathpeffer and Dingwall, Easter Ross. The mountain, 3,722 ft, is always topped with snow. The water for the distillery is brought through conduit 3½ miles from Loch Ussie. Belonged in 1887 to D. G. Ross. The Invergordon Distillers Ltd.

BLAIR ATHOL, Pitlochry, Perthshire, at the reputed geographical centre of Scotland. The distillery was built in 1826 by a Mr Conachar and taken over later in the century by P. Mackenzie & Co. The district was famous for whisky-making before the Act of 1823. Blair Athol won its renown with pure Highland malt whisky made with water direct from Ben Vrackie, pure, sparkling, clear and crystal. Arthur Bell & Sons Ltd. purchased the distillery in 1933. It is one of the most picturesque in Scotland. There are wonderful gardens. In the summer Pitlochry Pipe Band plays to entertain many of the thousands of visitors who annually visit this distillery. Parts of the premises have stood for more than 200 years. Among the romantic associations is an oak tree in which a fugitive from Prince Charlie's Highland Army hid before escaping to France. Arthur Bell & Sons Ltd.

CAPERDONICH, Rothes, Glengrant's second distillery, completely modernised in 1967 with highly automated plant. The Glenlivet & Glen Grant Distillers Ltd.

CARDOW, Knockando, Morayshire. Established as a licensed distillery in 1824, using water from the Mannoch Hill brought through two miles of pipe into the heart of the distillery. The same place yielded the peats for the drying of the green malt. It was owned at the end of the century by E. Cumming and had a big trade with Leith. Later it was acquired by John Walker & Sons Ltd.—Scottish Malt Distillers Ltd. (DCL).

CLYNELISH, Brora, Sutherland. On the north side of Strath Brora, 71 miles from Wick and 90 from Inverness. The Marquis of Stafford, afterwards the first Duke of Sutherland, founded the distillery in 1819 near Brora coalfield and his Dunrobin Castle. Ainslie & Heilbron (Distillers) Ltd. (DCL).

COLEBURN, Elgin, Morayshire. Founded in 1896. Jointly acquired by DCL and John Walker in 1915. J. & G. Stewart Ltd. (DCL).

CONVALMORE, Dufftown, dates from 1894. Scene of an experiment with the introduction of a patent still, with a capacity of 500 gallons of wash, in 1910. It proved that the products of the old pot-stills matured better, and the patent still was dismantled in 1916. The distillery was built in 1894 by Peter Dawson, grain merchant, Balvenie Mills. W. P. Lowrie & Co. Ltd. (DCL).

CRAGGANMORE, Ballindalloch, Inveravon, Banffshire. Built in 1869 by John Smith, facing the River Spey in front of Cragganmore Hill (1,600 ft). James Watson & Co., Scotch whisky merchants, Dundee, purchased its Highland malt whisky and marketed it last century. D. & J. McCallum Ltd. (DCL).

CRAIGELLACHIE, Banffshire. Built 1890, bought in 1924 by Mackie & Co., later White Horse Distillers Ltd. (DCL).

DAILUAINE, Carron, Strathspey, Banffshire. The name of the distillery in Gaelic means "green vale." It is situated on the banks of the Carron Burn, fed by water from the springs on Ben Rinnes. Built amid its cluster of trees early last century. In 1916 Dewar, DCL, W. P. Lowrie and John Walker combined to buy the company which operated it, Dailuaine-Talisker Distilleries Ltd. (DCL).

DALLAS DHU, Forres, Morayshire, a Lossieside distillery founded in 1899, Benmore Distilleries Ltd. (DCL).

DALMORE, Alness, Ross-shire. Established in 1839, another of the valuable Easter Ross distilleries, situated under a thickly wooded hill overlooking Cromarty Firth, on the River Alness, which runs from Loch Gildermoy near Ben Wyvis, believed to be the finest water procurable for distilling. Mackenzie Brothers owned it last century. They were keen farmers who grew vast quantities of barley on the Easter Ross plains and bred Aberdeen-Angus cattle and pedigree Clydesdale horses. In 1960 Mackenzie Brothers merged with Whyte & Mackay, makers of famous whiskies —Whyte & Mackay Special, Supreme and 21 Years Old. Mackenzie Bros, Dalmore, Ltd. (Harrods, House of Fraser).

DALWHINNIE, Inverness-shire, in the Drumochter Pass, highest distillery in Scotland. It was begun in the 1890s and acquired in 1905 by an American syndicate but eventually by the DCL's Scottish Malt Distillers Ltd. James Buchanan & Co. Ltd. (DCL).

DEANSTON, Doune, Perthshire. Deanston Distillers Ltd.

DUFFTOWN-GLENLIVET, Banffshire. The famous distillery town was founded by James Duff, 4th Earl of Fife, in 1817, which explains the name, a corruption of the Gaelic *dubh*, black, often applied as a description to dark-haired persons and eventually becoming a surname. The town is at the confluence of the Dullan and Fiddich Waters, the Dullan flowing down the limestone declivity of Ben Rinnes. The distillery was established in 1896 and was purchased by Bell's in 1933. Its supply of water comes from a famous well in the district—Jock's Well. The water is reckoned ideal for the manufacture of whisky. The Dufftown-Glenlivet, a typical Speyside malt, as well as being among the desirable singles, is extremely popular with blenders. Arthur Bell & Sons Ltd.

EDRADOUR, Pitlochry, Perthshire. The Gaelic name means "between two waters." The distillery was built in 1837 at the foot of a steep hill on ground rented from the Duke of Atholl and is near the ducal castle, Blair Atholl. William Whiteley Ltd. (Glenforres Distillery Co., famous for "House of Lords" and "King's Ransom" whiskies.)

FETTERCAIRN, Stonehaven, Kincardineshire. Actually the distillery is six miles from the town of Stonehaven. It was built in 1824 near the Esk, a river noted for salmon and scenery, and water of superior quality from the top of the Grampians. Its Highland malt early won markets in Glasgow and Leith. Fettercairn Distillery Ltd.

GLEN ALBYN, Inverness, capital of the Highlands. The name means the Glen of Scotland, and gives a suggestion of regal rank to this distillery founded in 1846 by Provost Sutherland. It was rebuilt by Gregory & Co. in 1884, at the side of the Caledonian Canal basin. Mackinlays & Birnie Ltd. (DCL).

GLENALLACHIE, Aberlour, Banffshire. Built in 1968. Mackinlay-McPherson Ltd. (Scottish & Newcastle Breweries).

GLENBURGIE-GLENLIVET, Rafford, Forres, Morayshire. Source of one of the highly recommended singles, this distillery was founded in 1810 by the grandfather of Dr Liston Paul, the London surgeon. It is one of the oldest distilleries in the North. James & George Stodart Ltd.—Hiram Walker & Sons (Scotland) Ltd.

41

GLENCADAM, Brechin, Angus. In the cleft of a hill half a mile from the cathedral city, this distillery draws splendid water from the Moorfoot Loch and uses local barley. Glencadam Distillery Co. was taken over in 1954 by Hiram Walker. George Ballantine & Son Ltd. (Hiram Walker).

GLENDRONACH, Huntly, Aberdeenshire, was once owned by Charles Grant, son and tunman to William Grant of Glenfiddich. Situated in the valley of the Forgue between Foreman and Coulsalmon hills, where the Dronach Burn runs over rich peat beds and mossy uplands before running through the distillery, this place was established in 1826 by James Allardyce and associates. It soon won renown for a malt whisky which tasted like liqueur. Glendronach Distillery Co. Ltd.—Teachers (Distillers) Ltd. acquired the interest in 1962.

GLENDULLAN, Dufftown, built by William Williams & Sons Ltd., Aberdeen. Macdonald Greenlees Ltd.

GLEN ELGIN, Elgin. White Horse Distillers Ltd. (DCL).

GLENFARCLAS-GLENLIVET, Ballindalloch, Banffshire. Established 1836 by J. & G. Grant Ltd. with water drawn from springs on Ben Rinnes.

GLENFIDDICH, Dufftown. Started by William Grant, a local man. He worked with Gordon and Cowie at Mortlach Distillery for some time before acquiring the plant of the old Cardow Distillery and building Glenfiddich in 1886, starting to distil the following year. The premises, including bottling plant, were greatly enlarged in 1955. Wm. Grant & Son Ltd.

GLEN GARIOCH, Old Meldrum, Aberdeenshire. Founded in 1797 by Ingram, Lamb & Co., sold by John Manson & Co. in 1840 to J. F. Thomson & Co., Leith. William Sanderson became co-owner in 1886. The water supply comes from Piercock Hill on the Meldrum House estate. The Glen Garioch Distillery Co. Ltd. (Stanley P. Morrison Ltd.).

GLENGLASSAUGH, Fordyce, Portsoy, Banffshire. Two miles from the port in fertile countryside near the Moray Firth, the distillery was established in 1875, built on the slope of a steep hill with pure water from the Knock Hills and Glassaugh River and the benefit of local barley of high quality. The Highland Distilleries Co. Ltd.

GLENGOYNE, Killearn, Stirlingshire. Lang Brothers Ltd.

GLENGRANT-GLENLIVET, Rothes. In 1840 the brothers J. and J. Grant moved their distillery here from Dandaleith, two and a half miles to the south, where they had been producing whisky since 1834. The famous barley-growing plains of Morayshire and the convenience of the mountain springs determined the brothers' choice of location. The distillery was considerably enlarged in 1865 and a second distillery was added in 1897–1901, and reopened and completely modernised in 1967. J. & J. Grant, Glen Grant, Ltd.

GLEN KEITH-GLENLIVET, Keith. Chivas Bros. Ltd., 1958.

GLENLIVET, The. On the fir-clad banks of Loch Park, the Smiths produced their supreme Highland malt whisky praised by Sir Walter Scott and James Hogg and ordered by King George IV on his State visit to Scotland in 1822. Lady Grant of Rothiemurchus acquired it for the monarch, and this pleased him so much that he appointed her father to an Indian judgeship. This is *brot an stuth*, the best of stuff, made with local barley, local peat, local hereditary skill. In 1880 Col. Smith of Glenlivet made a bid to restrain other distillers from using the name "Glenlivet" to designate their products. Now the product of this distillery is always preceded by the definite article and called distinctly "Smith's." George & J. G. Smith Ltd.

GLENLOCHY, Loch Lochy, Fort William. Scottish Malt Distillers Ltd. (DCL).

GLENLOSSIE, Elgin. The River Lossie, with its source in a small loch in the parish of Dallas runs twenty-six miles to the Moray Firth at Lossiemouth. The distillery is four miles out of Elgin and stands at the foot of a fir-clad hill in beautiful country with clear air. The sparkling water comes from a reservoir and a hill spring. In 1887 John Hopkins & Co., London and Glasgow, had sole sale of the product. The distillery owned by J. Duff & Co., Elgin, was acquired by Scottish Malt Distillers in 1919, and was the first in Morayshire to come under their organisation. John Haig & Co. Ltd. (DCL).

GLEN MHOR, Inverness. Named after the Great Glen of Scotland, traversed by the Caledonian Canal. Mackinlays & Birnie Ltd. (DCL).

GLENMORANGIE, Tain, Ross-shire. An old brewery, in existence since 1738, was converted to a distillery in 1843 by William Matheson in this spot, whose Gaelic name means "the big glen of the mound." Its Highland malt whisky found markets in England as well as Scotland last century. Macdonald & Muir Ltd.

GLEN MORAY-GLENLIVET, Elgin. 1893. Macdonald & Muir Ltd.

GLENROTHES-GLENLIVET, Rothes, built in 1878, went into production the night of the Tay Bridge Disaster, 28 December 1879. Founded by a Speyside syndicate—William Grant, banker, Elgin; Provost Robert Dick, banker, Rothes; and James Stuart, grain merchant. The Highland Distillers Co. Ltd.

GLEN SPEY, Rothes. Built in 1887 by James Stuart, grain merchant. W. & A. Gilbey Ltd. (International Distillers & Vintners).

GLENTAUCHERS, Botriphnie, Keith. 1898. James Buchanan & Co. Ltd. (DCL).

GLENTURRET, Crieff, Perthshire. One of the oldest distilleries in Scotland, dating back to 1775, in old smuggler country two miles from Crieff on the banks of the cascading River Turret which runs from Benchonzie (Kenneth's Mountain), 3,000 ft. Glenturret Distillery Ltd.

GLENUGIE, Peterhead, Aberdeenshire. Built in 1875 at the foot of a hill near the North Sea, drawing its barley from fertile Buchan and its soft, pure water from the mossy moorlands, first-rate for distilling and blending. Acquired in 1937 by Long John Distilleries Ltd. (Seager Evans & Co. Ltd.—Schenley Industries Inc., U.S.A.).

GLENURY-ROYAL, Stonehaven, Kincardineshire. Founded in 1836 by the gentleman athlete, marathon walker and trainer of Prize Ring champions, Captain Barclay Allardyce of Urie, the distillery is situated on the banks of the Cowie (broom) Burn, which flows through Glen Urie (Gleann Iubhraich, valley of the yew). The captain sold the distillery to William Ritchie. Benefits from pure local water and high quality barley from the same district. John Gillon & Co. Ltd.

HIGHLAND PARK, Kirkwall, Orkney. A famous name among whisky connoisseurs, the distillery was developed by Stuart and Mackay from two springs discovered at opposite ends of the park. James Grant & Co. (Highland Park Distillery) Ltd.

HILLSIDE, Montrose, Angus. Wm. Sanderson & Son Ltd.

IMPERIAL, Carron, Strathspey, Banffshire. One of the famous Speyside distilleries established by the Dailuaine-Talisker Distilleries Ltd. in 1897 and used for malting. Electric plant was installed in 1962. Dailuaine-Talisker Distilleries Ltd. (DCL).

INCHGOWER, Rathven, Fochabers. Originally the distillery was established at Tochieneal by Alexander Wilson, in 1822, but was moved by Alex. Wilson & Co. in 1871 to Inchgower ("goat pasture"). Fine distilling water from the Letter Burn flowing through the mossy uplands, and from the Aultmoor springs, determined the choice of site. Purchased in 1936 by Arthur Bell & Sons Ltd.

ISLE OF JURA, Argyll. Established in 1810 but existent in 18th century. Acquired by James Ferguson & Sons last century. Closed down in 1904, rebuilt in 1963. Isle of Jura Distillery Co. Ltd. (Mackinlay & McPherson Ltd.—Scottish & Newcastle Breweries).

KNOCKANDO, Morayshire. Named after a *cnocan dubh*, little black hill—the locals pronounce the *k*. The distillery was built in 1898 and acquired by W. & A. Gilbey Ltd. in 1900. It was the first Speyside distillery to have electric light, and introduced electric motors. Justerini & Brooks Ltd. (International Distillers & Vintners).

KNOCKDHU, Knock, Grange, Banffshire. This name also means a rounded black hill or knoll. First malt distillery built by DCL, 1893–4. James Munro & Son Ltd.

LEDAIG, Tobermory, Isle of Mull. An interesting revival. The Tobermory distillery was established in 1823 using water from the Tobermory River running past the site into the sea. Last century it was owned by Mackill Bros. and produced 62,000 gallons of "Mull whisky," pure Highland malt, annually. It ceased distilling in 1924 and closed down in 1933, and has recently been restarted by Mr James Morrison in association with Mr George A. Currie, an oil magnate; Domecq, the sherry company, and the Larringa Steamship Co. of Liverpool. The aim is to raise the output with two extra stills from 500,000 gallons to 800,000 gallons a year.

Scott described Tobermory in the days when the distillery was first starting: "The people were getting in their patches of corn; and the shrill voices of the children attending their parents in the field, and loading the little ponies which are used in transporting the grain, formed a chorus not disagreeable . . ." He quoted the judgment of Sacheverell, in 1688, that the bay of Tobermory might equal any prospect in Italy. Ledaig Distillery (Tobermory) Ltd.

LINKWOOD, St Andrews Llanbryd, Elgin, Morayshire. There was a distillery in the woods here in 1821. Rebuilt by William Brown, 1873. Acquired by Scottish Malt Distillers Ltd. in 1933. John McEwan & Co. Ltd. (DCL).

LOCH LOMOND, Dunbartonshire. Barton Distilling (Scotland) Ltd. (Barton Brands Inc., Chicago).

LOCHSIDE, Montrose, Angus. Macnab Distilleries Ltd.

LONGMORN-GLENLIVET, Elgin. The Longmorn-Glenlivet Distilleries Ltd.

MACALLAN-GLENLIVET, Elchies, Craigellachie. Established 1824, acquired by James Stuart & Co. last century, and formed into a limited liability company in 1946. R. Kemp, Macallan-Glenlivet Ltd.

MACDUFF, Deveron, Banff, Glendeveron Distilleries Ltd.

MANNOCHMORE, Birnie. John Haig & Co. Ltd. (DCL).

MILTONDUFF-GLENLIVET, Elgin. Long famed for "Creamy Old Milton Duff Whisky." Founded in 1824 by George Ballantine & Son Ltd. (Hiram Walker).

MORTLACH, Dufftown, Banffshire. Some believe the name to mean "great pleasure." Built 1823 by George Gordon and James Findlater. George Cowie took over in 1867 and his son, Dr A. M. Cowie, succeeded in 1897. In 1923 the doctor sold the business to John Walker & Sons Ltd. (Scottish Malt Distillers Ltd. since 1936). George Cowie & Son Ltd. (DCL).

NORTH PORT, Brechin, Angus. Brechin depended for its whisky on smugglers from the Grampians until in 1820 the three brothers David, John and Alexander Guthrie, brothers of Dr Thomas Guthrie, founder of the "Ragged School" for wayward boys, started a distillery, using piped water from the Grampians, peats from the uplands and the high quality barley of the area. Their company became Guthrie, Martin & Co. North Port is operated by Mitchell Bros. Ltd. (DCL).

OBAN, Argyll. The name means the little bay. In Gaelic it is properly *Oban Lathurna*, the little bay of Lorne. The distillery was built in 1794 by the Stevensons who converted Oban from a fishing village into a thriving town. Later acquired by Walter Higgin and noted for its good single Highland malt whisky. William Greer & Co. Ltd.

ORD, Muir-of-Ord, Ross-shire. Famous since last century for its single whisky produced from home-grown barley and fine water from Glen Oran, neighbouring lochs and a substantial reservoir. Ord Highland malt was known long ago as far away as Singapore. Peter Dawson Ltd (DCL).

PULTENEY, Wick, Caithness. Farthest north of the mainland distilleries and one of the oldest, established in 1826 by James Henderson who had already been distilling with success for twenty years farther inland. See "Old Pulteney" in the singles list. James & George Stodart Ltd, acquired by Hiram Walker in 1955.

ROYAL BRACKLA, Nairn. Built by Captain William Fraser in 1812 on the Cawdor Burn. Some time around 1835 the captain received an order from His Majesty's cellarman for a small cask of whisky to be sent to St James's Palace, so Brackla Highland malt became known as "The King's Whisky." Scottish Malt Distillers since 1890. John Bisset & Co. Ltd (DCL).

ROYAL LOCHNAGAR, Balmoral. John Begg Ltd (DCL).

SCAPA, Kirkwall, Orkney. Built on the Lingrow Burn at the head of Scapa Bay, taking its water supply from the burn and nearby springs, completed in 1885 by Macfarlane & Townsend. Hiram Walker took over in 1965. Taylor & Ferguson Ltd.

SPEYBURN, Rothes. John Robertson & Son Ltd (DCL).

SPEYSIDE, Kingussie. Speyside Distillery Co. Ltd.

STRATHISLA-GLENLIVET, Keith. Milton Distillery was founded in Keith in 1786 by George Taylor, banker, postmaster, flax-dresser and distiller; later owned by John McDonald, saddler; purchased by William Longmore; acquired in the Second World War by Chivas Bros, Aberdeen, enlarged and renamed. Chivas Brothers Ltd (Joseph Seagram & Sons—Samuel Bronfman).

STRATHMILL, Keith. Built at a former mill in 1892, taken over by Gilbeys and greatly expanded in 1895. Introduced the first whisky tanker, "Whisky Galore," to transport its Highland malt to the blenders. Justerini & Brooks Ltd. (International Distillers & Vintners).

TALISKER, Carbost, Isle of Skye. On the shore of Loch Harport at the foot of a hill. Acquired 1916 by Dewar, Distillers Company Limited, W. P. Lowrie and John Walker. Dailuaine-Talisker Distilleries Ltd (DCL).

TAMDHU-GLENLIVET, Knockando, Morayshire. The place-name is properly *tom dubh*, a black, barrow-like hill, but it has become Doricised to Tam, the Lowland Scots pronunciation of the name Tom or Thomas. The distillery, established 1897, was acquired by The Highland Distilleries Ltd, and equipped with electric machinery and Saladin malting plant.

TAMNAVULIN-GLENLIVET, Tomnavoulin, Banffshire. A real Speyside distillery, high in the hills. Tamnavulin-Glenlivet Distillery Co. Ltd.

TEANANINCH, Alness, Ross-shire. Once owned by J. McGilchrist Ross, across the river from Dalmore Distillery, and built up on the virtues of a rich and fertile hinterland. R. H. Thomson & Co. (Distillers) Ltd.

TOMATIN, Inverness-shire. A few miles south of the Highland capital, producing a peaty but light Highland malt whisky. Tomatin Distillers Co. Ltd.

TOMINTOUL-GLENLIVET, Ballindalloch. The Tomintoul-Glenlivet Distillery Ltd.

TORMORE, Advie. Built in 1958-9, designed by Sir A. E. Richardson, PPRA, in consultation with Col. A. Cullen, OBE, Inverness. Of Kemnay granite, this complex of distillery, cooperage, storage warehouses and ten houses is a complete distillery and village on the most modern lines. Long John Distilleries Ltd (Schenley Industries Inc., U.S.A.).

TULLIBARDINE, Blackford, Perthshire. Near the sources of Allan Water, the remains of Ogilvie Castle, Gleneagles and the Pass through the Ochils to Rumbling Bridge. Tullibardine Distillery Ltd.

## THE ISLAY MALT DISTILLERIES

Although Islay is very much part of Gaeldom, its malt whiskies are named separately from the Highland malts, although these include the products of other islands—Mull, Skye, Jura (near Islay) and Orkney. Islay (pronounced Ile-ah) is a fertile island which almost always looks in good fettle. It sustains fine cattle. Peat is part of its natural wealth and traditionally this has been cut for the distilleries.

Islay malt whisky has a distinctive peat-reek flavour, and some say it even has the tang of seaweed. Certainly the distilleries hug the sea shore and its distillers have always been believers in the efficacy of the sea air in good malting. Although strong, the flavour of Islay malt is always pleasant, and the whiskies from here are popular with blenders as well as with the connoisseurs of single whiskies.

ARDBEG. Founded by McDougalls of Ardbeg, 1815, situated on the south-east corner of the island overlooking the sea. Original owners, Alexander McDougall & Co. Ardbeg Distillery Ltd.

BOWMORE. On the sea shore, with good water from the Laggan, the island's best and largest river. Sheriff's Bowmore Distillery Ltd (associated with Stanley P. Morrison Ltd, whisky brokers, Glasgow).

BRUICHLADDICH (*bruach chladaich*, bank of the shore), on Lochindaal; built in 1881. Bruichladdich Distillery Co. Ltd.

BUNNAHABHAIN (the name means "riverfoot"), in the north-east of the island, facing Jura. Built in 1881 to meet the growing demand for Islay malt whisky. The Highland Distilleries Co. Ltd.

CAOL ILA ("Strait of Islay") overlooks the narrows south of Bruichladdich, and two miles north of Port Askaig, looking over at the Paps of Jura. Water from Torrabus Loch said to be the finest in Islay. The distillery was built in 1846. Bulloch Lade & Co. Ltd (DCL).

LAGAVULIN ("hollow of the mill"), from 1835 belonged to J. L. Mackie & Co. and was managed by J. C. Graham, resident partner. Used water from the cascading Lagavulin stream. White Horse Distillers Ltd (DCL).

LAPHROAIG, built on the sea shore a mile from Port Ellen in 1820 by D. Johnston & Co. Source of a single and base of the blend "Islay Mist." D. Johnston & Co. (Laphroaig) Ltd (Seager Evans).

PORT ELLEN ("the port of the island"), the distillery is on the sea shore half a mile from the town, built 1825, much enlarged since, used for storage. Low, Robertson & Co. Ltd (DCL).

## CAMPBELTOWN MALT WHISKIES

Campbeltown in Kintyre (*ceann tire*, end of the land), the peninsula which stretches almost to touch Ireland, was at one time a town of many distilleries. Now it has two. They use Scottish or English barley as available and suitable for quality, augmented by imported barley when necessary. The malt whisky produced here is sent by road to blenders. Local farmers appreciate the wet draff which is a by-product of the whisky-making. The single whiskies are well worth acquiring.

GLEN SCOTIA. Built in 1832 by Stewart, Galbraith & Co., to exploit clear water from Crosshill Loch and eighty-foot deep rock wells. A. Gillies & Co. (Distillers) Ltd.

SPRINGBANK. Founded in 1826 by the Mitchell family, also with water from Crosshill Loch. Its whisky was famous in London and Glasgow a century ago. In 1973 Springbank Campbeltown Malt Whisky won the championship award at the International Wine and Spirit Fair at Ljubljana, Yugoslavia, competing against spirits of all kinds and liqueurs from many nations. Thrice winner of the gold medal at Ljubljana, it was the first Scotch whisky to win the crowning champion's award. J. & A. Mitchell & Co. Ltd.

## LOWLAND MALT WHISKIES

Lowlands, as used in Scotland, is a misleading term if it conveys the idea of low-lying country such as the Netherlands. The Lowlands of Scotland are mostly quite hilly. There are plenty of conditions suitable for distilling, even of malt whisky, in the Lowlands, which are rich in good water and even have peat, and also have good clean air and the proper temperature and humidity for whisky-making.

AUCHENTOSHAN, Dalmuir, Old Kilpatrick, Dunbartonshire. On the north bank of the Clyde, almost in Glasgow, but really on the boundary line of the Highlands, and near the reputed birthplace of St Patrick, the distillery was founded in 1825 to use the fine quality water from Cochna Loch in the Kilpatrick Hills. C. H. Curtis & Co. of Greenock were the owners last century. Eadie Cairns Ltd.

BLADNOCH, near Wigtown, in the South-West of Scotland and on the Solway Firth which separates England from Scotland, was founded in 1817 by John and Thomas McClelland and later carried on, enlarged and modernised, by Charles McClelland. Bladnoch Distillery Co. Ltd.

GLENKINCHIE, Pencaitland, East Lothian, south-east of Edinburgh in the glen of the Kinchie, a tributary of the River Tyne which flows into the Firth of Forth. To the south are the Lammermuir Hills which reach heights of 2,000 feet. The hinterland is richly agricultural. Glenkinchie has long produced a sweet and palatable Scotch Lowland malt whisky. The distillery on the Kinchie Burn is one of the most up-to-date in the country and its whisky, because of the pure water used and other virtues, is ideal for blending. John Haig & Co. Ltd (DCL).

GLEN FOYLE, Gargunnock, Stirlingshire. Gargunnock's name is Welsh for a conical fort, near the Fintry Hills and the Endrick Water. Built 1826 by A. Chrystal and John McNee, taken over in 1880 by James Calder & Co. Water from Campsie Fells. Brodie Hepburn Ltd.

INVERLEVEN, Dumbarton, also on the Highland boundary. Dumbarton means the fort of the Britons, and it marked the bounds of the old British kingdom of Strathclyde against the encroachments of the Scots who had settled in Argyll. Hiram Walker & Sons (Scotland) Ltd.

LITTLEMILL, Bowling, Dunbartonshire, twelve miles from Glasgow on the north bank of the Clyde. The distillery was built in 1800 and enlarged in 1875 by William Hay, using peat from Stornoway, Isle of Lewis, and from Perthshire, and water from a sequestered glen high in the Kilpatrick Hills, collected in a reservoir. Its whisky was famous long ago even in India and the Colonies. Barton Distilling (Scotland) Ltd. (Barton Brands Inc., Chicago).

LOMOND, Dumbarton. Could there be a better name for a distillery producing Scotch malt whisky, than one taken from the nearby "Bonnie, Bonnie Banks of Loch Lomond"? Hiram Walker & Sons (Scotland) Ltd. (Gooderman & Worts Ltd.).

ROSEBANK, Falkirk, Stirlingshire. A very old distillery, where whisky was being made in 1798 by Stark Bros. In 1840 James Rankine began here as a distiller. In 1864 the plant was entirely rebuilt by R. W. Rankine. See the list of singles. The Distillers Agency Ltd (DCL).

ST MAGDALENE, Linlithgow, near the birthplace of Mary Queen of Scots. This distillery is familiar to all rail travellers passing through the old regal town. Built on lands of St Magdalene's Cross by Sebastian Henderson. John Hopkins & Co. Ltd (DCL).

MOFFAT, Airdrie, Lanarkshire. Near Glasgow. Inver House Distilleries Ltd. (Publicker Industries Inc., Philadelphia).

The distilleries marked DCL are run by Scottish Malt Distillers Ltd—Glenkinchie, Rosebank and St Magdalene since 1914, Glenlossie since 1919 and North Port Distillery, Brechin, since 1922 and many others since 1930, with Linkwood added in 1933.

The stillhouse at Ord Distillery, Muir-of-Ord, Ross-shire, famous for its Ord Highland Malt whisky.

*Above*
The blending hall at Barleith, Kilmarnock. Here the many single whiskies combined in Johnnie Walker are sampled and then "disgorged" into the the stainless steel channels which flow into the 42,000 gallon blending vat.

*Left*
At Glen Elgin Distillery, Longmuir, Morayshire, the resident Excise Officer watches the filling of new whisky into casks for maturing.

# 4 The Grain Distilleries

SCOTCH GRAIN whisky distilleries number about a dozen, but are usually on a larger scale than the malt distilleries, and combine warehousing, research and other activities. Five of them are operated by Scottish Grain Distillers Limited, an offshoot of The Distillers Company Limited, who operate also a number of warehouse units in other parts. Four distilleries—Cambus, Cameronbridge, Carsebridge and Port Dundas—were acquired at the inauguration of DCL in 1877. The fifth, Caledonian Distillery in Edinburgh, followed in the 1880s.

They are located near main roads and railways in the Industrial Belt or Central Lowlands of Scotland, stretching from Clydeside to the Forth Valley. This has been described as "the cradle of DCL." The largest group of warehouses in Scotland is operated by Scottish Grain Distillers Limited in Clackmannanshire, dating from 1959. The policy is to site the newer warehouses in country spots away from built-up areas and to provide them with all the latest precautions against fire risks.

Here is an alphabetical list of the Scotch grain whisky distilleries, mainly, but not all, situated in the Lowlands:

BEN NEVIS, Fort William, already noted under malt distilleries, produces grain whisky as well as malt for blending. Built in 1878 by Donald P. McDonald, who in 1856 succeeded his father in the only licensed distillery in the district. Its water supply came from "Buchan's Well," the highest well in the United Kingdom. The old distillery was enlarged from time to time to meet the demand for "Long John's Dew of Ben Nevis," and eventually a new distillery had to be built. Ben Nevis Distillery (Fort William) Ltd.

CALEDONIAN, Edinburgh. At one time the capital of Scotland boasted several distilleries, including the Edinburgh Distillery of Andrew Usher & Co. in Sciennes St, which began as a brewery in the 14th century, was established as a malt distillery in 1849 and introduced the practice of blending different distillations. The Caledonian Distillery, Dalry Road, in the West End of the city, was built in 1855 by Menzies & Co. The Distillers Company Limited took it over in 1884, and it became the second largest distillery in the United Kingdom and a model for European distilleries, pioneering in every technological development. It is situated on the main railway lines near Haymarket Station and is convenient also to the Union Canal. Scottish Grain Distillers Ltd (DCL).

CAMBUS, Clackmannanshire. Founded in 1806 by John Mowbray, this grew from a small distillery in a very old mill, to one of great scale. In 1877 it became part of The Distillers Company Limited, of which Robert Mowbray of the Cambus Distillery was one of the founders. Scottish Grain Distillers Ltd (DCL).

CAMERONBRIDGE, Windygates, Fife. In 1810, John Haig of Cameron Bridge was producing a well-known Fife whisky, and in 1824 he took over Cameron Mill and built a new distillery, also taking out a licence to produce his whisky legally, a process which cost £10 under the new Act. By 1877 he was producing a quarter of a million gallons a year. Robert Stein's patent still accelerated the process. Haig installed it here in 1827 and erected the Coffey Still at Cameron Bridge in 1831. Cameron Bridge became one of the DCL's largest grain distilleries. Haig moved the blending to Markinch. The first yeast by-product was made for DCL at Cameron Bridge. Scottish Grain Distillers Ltd (DCL).

CARSEBRIDGE, Alloa, Clackmannanshire, about a mile from the town and built about 1799 as a malt distillery by John Bald of Carsebridge (John Bald & Co.). It changed over to grain about 1840, drawing its water from a mile-wide reservoir and turning out over two million gallons of pure grain whisky annually before the end of the century. John Bald of Carsebridge was one of the founders of DCL in 1877. Scottish Grain Distillers Ltd (DCL).

DUMBARTON. Prominently situated near Dumbarton Rock on the north bank of the Clyde estuary, this to the visitor to Scotland is probably the best known distillery in the land, though it came on to our landscape only in 1937 in response to the quickened demand for Scotch whisky with the repeal of the Volstead Amendment to the United States Constitution. A large firm of Canadian distillers saw the wisdom of building their own distillery in Scotland. They bought the site of McMillan's shipyard at Dumbarton, filled in the dock and erected factory and plant at a cost of half a million pounds. The building was then one of the tallest in Scotland, fourteen storeys high in front, though there have been many high buildings erected on Clydeside since that time. The company has since expanded its activities well beyond this original enterprise. Hiram Walker & Sons (Scotland) Ltd.

GARNHEATH, Airdrie, belongs to Publicker Industries Inc., Philadelphia 2, Pa, U.S.A.

GIRVAN, Ayrshire. A £1¼ million grain distillery opened in 1962 by Wm Grant & Sons Ltd.

INVERGORDON, Ross-shire. A grain distillery right in the northern Highlands, in Easter Ross near Dingwall and Strathpeffer, an area which is now booming industrially. The Invergordon Distillers Ltd.

LOCHSIDE, Montrose. Macnab Distilleries Ltd.

MOFFAT, Airdrie, Inver House Distilleries Ltd, a subsidiary of Publicker of Philadelphia.

NORTH BRITISH, Edinburgh. Dates from 1888. North British Distillery Co. Ltd.

NORTH OF SCOTLAND, Cambus, Clackmannanshire. North of Scotland Distilling Co. Ltd.

PORT DUNDAS, Glasgow. A very early distillery was begun here in the 18th century by Robert Macfarlane, and last century it became one of the largest in the world with an output of 2½ million gallons a year. Daniel and Robert Macfarlane of M. Macfarlane & Co., Port Dundas Distillery, took part in the formation of The Distillers Company Limited in 1877. The distillery is situated on the Forth and Clyde Canal. Scottish Grain Distillers Ltd (DCL.)

STRATHCLYDE, Glasgow. Long John Distilleries Ltd (Schenley Industries Inc., U.S.A.).

# 5    Single Whiskies

IF YOU wish to be a thorough snob about Scotch, you will want to confine your drinking almost entirely to the malt whiskies, and to talk learnedly of single, individual or self whiskies. There are fanatical Speysiders—the Wee Frees of whisky tasting—who think that blending is the work of the Devil. But there are many discerning Scotch whisky drinkers who appreciate good proprietary brands.

There are about a dozen malt whiskies that you ought to taste whenever you have the opportunity. Each of them is an experience. They are not easy to procure everywhere. Barmen may tell you: "We don't stock it. Nobody here ever asks for it." You may pub-crawl over an entire city in search of Glenmorangie or Talisker, without success, then one enchanted evening, across the crowded room, you will see it smiling . . .

You will find The Glenlivet (Smith's) here and there by happy chance—"serendipity" is the classical word. But you will also stray into deserts where it is unobtainable. Glenfiddich also is something one is lucky to discover away from familiar territory. If you are a malt drinker you will find knowing the pubs as important as carrying a mental map of all the loos in town. But the same applies to some good proprietary brands, which may be as local in their incidence as the weather.

There are connoisseurs' lists of malts, including the ones I have mentioned, along with Glen Grant, Glen Burgie-Glenlivet, Cardow, Balmenach, Old Pulteney, Highland Park, Royal Brackla, Longmorn-Glenlivet, Macallan-Glenlivet, Linkwood, Clynelish and Glenlossie. The experts would disagree about the order in which they should be placed, but I have named the top fifteen. Here is a check list of the malts available, and while you are on the singles-tasting lark, try to acquire also the single grain whisky, Cameron Bridge, from John Haig & Co. Ltd, Markinch, Fife.

With the growing demand for single malt whiskies, it is likely that more of these will be released for general circulation. In the meantime the following alphabetical list describes those available:

## ABERLOUR-GLENLIVET

Distilled at Aberlour, Banffshire, by Aberdour-Glenlivet Distillery Co. This eight-years-old, 100° proof, light-bodied malt, distinctively flavoured in the Speyside style, has been popular for some years on the Italian market and is being introduced on the home front.

## ARDBEG

Distilled on the Isle of Islay by Ardbeg Distillery Ltd, 175 West George Street, Glasgow. A dram from the seaside with the distinctive Islay tang, peaty and appetising, 8 years old.

## AUCHENTOSHAN

Distilled at Dalmuir, Dunbartonshire, by Eadie Cairns Ltd, 11 Bothwell Street, Glasgow. This is a pleasant full-bodied Lowland malt from the distillery situated near St Patrick's reputed birthplace on the north bank of the River Clyde as it opens out to the estuary. Auchentoshan has been distilled for almost 150 years from the best selected barley and the fine water of the Kilpatrick Hills.

## AULTMORE

Distilled at Keith, Banffshire, by John and Robert Harvey & Co. Ltd, 5 Oswald Street, Glasgow, C.1, a company in the DCL group. Coming from a rich centre of whisky production, this lovely Speyside Highland malt single is eminently drinkable at 12 years of age.

## BALBLAIR

Distilled at Edderton, Ross-shire, by Balblair Distillery Co. Ltd. (Hiram Walker & Sons (Scotland) Ltd). Redolent of the "parish of peats" which is its hinterland, but not overpoweringly so. A pleasant and quite distinctive drink.

## BALVENIE

Distilled at Dufftown, Banffshire, by Wm Grant & Sons. Bottled 100° proof, 11 years old, a typical Speyside malt for the enthusiast. Bottled at 106.4° proof by Macfarlane Bruce & Co.

## BLADNOCH

Distilled at Wigtown by Bladnoch Distillery Ltd, 5 Claremont Terrace, Glasgow G3 7XR. A Lowland malt from close to the English Border, but like all Borderers, defiantly Scotch. A fragrant and inspiring dram, coming back into circulation.

## BLAIR ATHOL

Distilled at Pitlochry by Arthur Bell & Sons Ltd, Perth. It comes from the geographical centre of Scotland and the home of the Festival Theatre, and is made from the pure spring water of Ben Vrackie and from the best selected barley dried by peat. It is redolent of the grand Highland territory from which it emanates, and is a most satisfying drink.

## BOWMORE

Distilled on the Island of Islay by Sherriff's Bowmore Distillery Ltd. This a characteristically opulent Islay malt. It has the distinct peat-reek bouquet and the caressing, full-bodied maltiness. It is obtainable from the well-known whisky brokers, Stanley P. Morrison Ltd, 13 Royal Crescent, Glasgow, C.3.

## BRUICHLADDICH

Distilled on the Isle of Islay by The Invergordon Distillers Ltd, Invergordon, Ross-shire. A heartsome island malt, lingering like a warm kiss from an Islay lass.

## CAPERDONICH

Distilled at Rothes, Speyside, by The Glenlivet and Glen Grant Distillers Ltd. This is a charming example of the true Speyside product, 8 years old, peaty but pleasant and always a heart-warming and substantial drink. From J. & J. Grant (Glen Grant) Ltd, Glen Grant Distillery, Rothes, Morayshire.

## CARDHU

Distilled at Cardow, Knockando, Morayshire, by John Walker & Sons Ltd, Kilmarnock. This was a favourite of the connoisseur of whiskies, Aeneas Macdonald, an appealing Speyside Highland malt which has recently become available from Walker, one of the "Big Five" firms of the DCL grouping. At 12 years of age, Cardhu conveys the sweetness of the Mannoch Hill water and the fragrance of the moorland peats acting on carefully chosen barley in the best condition and maturing in the Highland air.

## CLYNELISH

Distilled at Brora, Sutherland, by Ainslie & Heilbron (Distillers) Ltd, 5 Oswald Street, Glasgow, C.1. A grand Highland malt which the connoisseurs place in the top twelve for full body, mildness, mellowness and tasteful flavour. Available at both 70° and 80° proof and 12 years of age, also at 90° proof, 15 years old.

## DALMORE

Distilled at Alness, Ross-shire, by Mackenzie Bros, Dalmore, Ltd (Whyte & Mackay Ltd). Not too peaty but an amicable malt, available at both 70° and 75° proof, 12 and even 20 years old.

## DEANSTON

Distilled at Doune, Perthshire, by Deanston Distillers Ltd. Not widely available.

## GLENBURGIE-GLENLIVET

Distilled at Forres by James and George Stodart Ltd, 3 High Street, Dumbarton. This delightful Speyside single, strong but gentlemanly, was among the dozen most highly recommended by the famous Highland malt expert, Aeneas Macdonald. From a distillery over 160 years old, it bears the label of a good old firm now part of the Hiram Walker empire.

## GLENDEVERON

Distilled at Macduff by Brodie Hepburn Ltd and bottled by Block, Grey & Block, London, at 75° proof, 5 years old. Not too peaty but a good Speyside malt.

## GLENDRONACH-GLENLIVET

Distilled at Huntly, Aberdeenshire, by Glendronach Distillery Co. Ltd, Glendronach, Forgue, Huntly. A Speysider that tastes like a liqueur from the distillery once owned by Charles of the famous Grant distilling family, it now has behind it the impeccable judgment of Wm Teacher & Sons Ltd, 14 St Enoch Square, Glasgow, C.1.

## GLENDULLAN

Distilled at Dufftown, Banffshire, by Macdonald Greenlees Ltd, 5 Maritime Street, Leith, Edinburgh EH6 6SF. A rich Speyside Highland malt whisky which is bottled at 82.3° proof, 12 years old, and makes a most equable and satisfying drink.

## GLENFARCLAS-GLENLIVET

Distilled at Ballindalloch by J. & G. Grant Ltd, Glenfarclas-Glenlivet Distillery, Marypark, Glendalloch, Banffshire. Peaty and palatable, this now popular Speysider has a pleasant and enduring appeal. It is still distilled by the firm which established it with Banffshire barley and peat and the water of Ben Rinnes about 140 years ago. Bottled 8 years old, 70°, 100° and 105° proof, and 12 years old, 70° proof.

## GLENFIDDICH

Distilled at Glenfiddich by William Grant & Sons. One of the great malts, at 8 years old, also obtainable over 10 years old. Quite peaty but a deeply satisfying dram.

### GLEN GARIOCH

Distilled in Old Meldrum, Aberdeenshire, by The Glen Garioch Distillery Co. Ltd. An ancient Highland malt recently made available, tasty and fragrant with just the hint of peat reek, light but lingering.

### GLENGOYNE

Distilled at Killearn, Stirlingshire, by Lang Bros Ltd, 100 West Nile Street, Glasgow, C.1 (one of the companies associated with Robertson & Baxter Ltd and the Highland Distilleries Co. Ltd). A pleasant single Highland malt from just on the Highland Line but with the full body and rich bouquet associated with the land of bens, glens and heroes, bottled at 8 years of age.

### GLEN GRANT-GLENLIVET

Distilled at Rothes by J. & J. Grant, Glen Grant, Ltd, Glen Grant Distillery, Rothes, Morayshire. High on the list of desirable, fragrant and delectable singles. Its clear, light colour proves that colour has little to do with the quality of a whisky beyond acting as trademark. It is available bottled at 100° proof, also at 5 years, 10 years and 15 years of age.

### GLEN ILA

Distilled at Caol Ila on the Island of Islay by Bulloch Lade & Co. Ltd, 75 Hope Street, Glasgow, C.2. A deliciously full-bodied and inspiring single Islay malt which is for export and a credit to Scotland and its island of origin.

### GLENMORANGIE

Distilled at Tain, Ross-shire, by Macdonald & Muir Ltd, Queen's Dock, Leith, Edinburgh EH6 6NN. Many discerning Scotch whisky drinkers place this at the head of their list of favourites, and some will drink nothing else. At 70° proof, 12 years old, it is as charming, old-world and interesting as its place of origin.

### GLENROTHES-GLENLIVET

Distilled at Rothes by The Highland Distillery Co. Ltd. A full and friendly Speyside Highland malt bottled at 80° proof, 10 years of age, this single has many devoted followers in all parts of the world. Also 8 years and 20 years old.

## GLEN SCOTIA

Distilled at Campbeltown, Kintyre, by A. Gillies & Co. Ltd, Newton Place, Glasgow. A pleasant Campbeltown malt whisky (there are only two left, alas) with the smoke of the peat and the kiss of good barley malt in it. Not widely available.

## GLENTURRET

Distilled at Crieff, Perthshire, by Glenturret Distillery Ltd. An unusual Highland malt from the old territory of the secret distillers and whisky smugglers. Not widely available.

## HIGHLAND PARK

Distilled at Kirkwall, Orkney by James Grant & Co. (Highland Park Distillery) Ltd. One of the famous Highland malt whiskies with the fragrance of peat and heather and a suggestion of rare brandy in its sip.

## INCHGOWER

Distilled at Buckie, Banffshire, by Arthur Bell & Sons Ltd, Perth. A splendid Highland malt matured near the sea in a healthy environment, and a heartsome dram, 12 years old. As the Buckie man said: "Wi' me, it'll nae grow muckle aulder." ("It won't grow much older"—as he intended to drink it there and then.)

## ISLE OF JURA

Distilled on the Island of Jura by the Isle of Jura Distillery Co. Ltd (Chas. Mackinlay & Co. Ltd, 111 Holyrood Road, Edinburgh EH8 8AY). Here is an attractive recent addition to the list of palatable single Highland malt whiskies recently made available (August 1973) by a grand old Leith firm of distillers and blenders now part of the Scottish & Newcastle Breweries Ltd group.

## LAGAVULIN

Distilled on the Island of Islay by White Horse Distillers Ltd, 120 St Vincent Street, Glasgow, C.2. At 75° proof, a piquantly peaty, pleasantly potable Islay malt, which, tasted as single, gives a clue to where White Horse gets its elegance as well as its kick. Sir Peter Mackie ("Restless Peter") trained as a distiller at Lagavulin and remained faithful to its Islay malt when he devised White Horse, giving that famous blend part of its distinction.

## LAPHROAIG

Distilled on the Island of Islay by D. Johnston & Co. (Laphroaig) Ltd, Laphroaig Distillery, Port Ellen, Islay. A famous Islay malt, full, strong and peaty in the island style and a delectable drink. Obtainable as a single at 75° proof, 10 years old, and a notable addition to the connoisseur's cellar. Supplied by Seager Evans & Co. Ltd, 20 Queen Anne's Gate, Westminster, London S.W.1, in conjunction with Long John Distilleries Ltd.

## LINKWOOD

Distilled at Elgin, Morayshire, by John McEwan & Co. Ltd (Low, Robertson & Co. Ltd, 10 Links Place, Leith, Edinburgh EH6 7HA). A pure Highland malt, a potent and palatable potion, bottled by the "Abbot's Choice" firm (DCL) at 70° and 75° proof, 12 years old.

## LITTLEMILL

Distilled at Bowling, Dunbartonshire, by Barton Distilling (Scotland) Ltd, Alexandria, Vale of Leven, Dunbartonshire. A charming Lowland malt from just on the Highland Line, scarce but available at 75° proof.

## LONGMORN-GLENLIVET

Distilled at Elgin, Morayshire, by The Longmorn-Glenlivet Distilleries Ltd. Local spring water and peat from Mannoch Hill go to the making of this fragrant dram, in which the "Queen Anne" firm of Hill Thomson, Frederick Street, Edinburgh, and the Glen Grant-Glenlivet group have an interest. A pleasant post-prandial draught.

## MACALLAN

Distilled at Macallan-Glenlivet Distillery, Craigellachie, by R. Kemp, Macallan-Glenlivet Ltd. This is one of the great Highland malts which Aeneas Macdonald places in his top twelve. It can be obtained bottled at 100° proof, 15 years old.

## MILTONDUFF-GLENLIVET

Distilled at Elgin by George Ballantine & Son Ltd, 2 Castle Street, Dumbarton. The true descendant of the widely admired

19th century "Creamy Old Milton Duff Whisky," this intriguing liqueur-like single malt retains that richness and satisfying strength. The discerning Hiram Walker & Sons (Scotland) Ltd, appreciative of the best in Scotch whiskies and especially Highland malts, acquired control of this outstanding Morayshire product of 150 years reputation, marketed under the name of the founding firm, which became part of the Hiram Walker grouping in 1954.

## MORTLACH

Distilled at Dufftown by George Cowie & Son Ltd, this Speyside Highland malt lives up to its Gaelic name (*mor-tlachd*, great delight) with its satisfying strength and peaty savour. William Grant of the famous Speyside family trained with Gordon & Cowie at Mortlach from 1866.

## OBAN

Distilled at Oban, Argyll, by William Greer & Co. Ltd. There is an Argyllshire charm, warmth and hospitality in the tasteful tang and strong friendliness of this truly Highland malt from the shore of the Firth of Lorne by the Atlantic Ocean. It is marketed by the DCL firm of John Hopkins & Co. Ltd, 5 Oswald Street, Glasgow, C.1.

## OLD FETTERCAIRN

Distilled at Fettercairn by Fettercairn Distillery Ltd, Stirrat Street, Paisley, this delectable drink is made from the best selected barley and Kincardineshire peats with the water of the Grampian Mountains and is a well attested favourite for 150 years.

## OLD PULTENEY

Distilled at Wick by James & George Stodart Ltd, 3 High Street, Dumbarton. This is one of the outstanding and well-loved Highland malt whiskies and comes from the far North in Caithness. It was a favourite of the author exciseman, the late Neil Gunn, who belonged to the area. It is strong and rewarding with a lingering flavour and a warming effect. The distillery came under the control of Hiram Walker & Sons (Scotland) Ltd in 1955.

## ORD

Distilled at Muir-of-Ord, Ross-shire, by Peter Dawson Ltd, Trafalgar House 75 Hope Street, Glasgow, C.2. Bottled at 76° proof, this world-renowned Highland malt whisky is reckoned by the soundest judges to be one of the best. It comes from near Beauly, the clan seat of the Frasers, has been famous from last century and made its markets right across the world to the Far East. Heather as well as peat was used in drying the barley.

## ROSEBANK

Distilled at Falkirk by The Distillers Agency Ltd, 7 Coates Crescent, Edinburgh EH3 7AB. A pleasantly smooth but strong Lowland malt from a distillery which has been in operation for 180 years.

## SPRINGBANK

Distilled at Campbeltown, Kintyre, by J. & A. Mitchell & Co· Ltd, Springbank Distillery, Campbeltown, Argyll. A Campbeltown malt which was famous early last century and has been winning international awards up to the present time. It was declared champion at Ljubljana in competition with spirits from all countries. At 80° proof, over 12 years old, this sprightly Spring Camp malt maintains its long-established distinction—Eaglesome Ltd.

## STRATHISLA

Distilled at Keith, Banffshire, by Chivas Bros Ltd, 111/113 Renfrew Road, Paisley. Strathisla means the valley of the Isla, the river that runs through the tweed and whisky Banffshire town of Keith, and this appetising and inspiringly full-flavoured and fragrant Highland malt whisky comes from the Strathisla-Glenlivet distillery. The Aberdeen firm of Chivas Bros acquired the famous 18th century distillery in World War II and later the business merged with Joseph Seagram & Sons, in the empire of the American Samuel Bronfman.

## TALISKER

Distilled on the Isle of Skye by Dailuaine-Talisker Distilleries Ltd. Aeneas Macdonald swayed between this peaty but light 8 years old Skye malt and the Sutherland Clynelish in rounding off his top twelve of distinguished whiskies. Many shrewd drinkers would have put it in, in preference to some of the others he chose without hesitation. Dailuaine-Talisker Distilleries is a DCL subsidiary. Talisker was acquired by the company in 1916 in association with Dewar, W. P. Lowrie and John Walker. It is a most desirable drink and is available at 70°, 80° and 100° proof.

## TAMDHU-GLENLIVET

Distilled at Knockando, Morayshire, by The Highland Distilleries Co. Ltd (agents, Robertson & Baxter Ltd, 106 West Nile Street, Glasgow). Tasty, slightly peaty, much in demand abroad and so not easy to find at home. A winsome Speysider playing hard to get, but bottled at Aberdeen by William Cadenhead.

## THE DUFFTOWN-GLENLIVET

Distilled in Dullan Glen, Dufftown, Banffshire, by Arthur Bell & Sons Ltd, Perth. A real Speyside Highland malt whisky much used in the making of reliable blends and highly desirable as a single, made from the water of "Jock's Well" and well-picked peat-dried barley by distillers of distinction. Eight years old, a wholesome malt, bottled at 80° proof.

## THE GLENLIVET

Distilled at Glenlivet, Banffshire, by George and J. G. Smith Ltd. Regarded by many experts as the premier malt whisky of Scotland, The Glenlivet (Smith's) is certainly a heart-warming beverage to encounter and one to which the drinker of Highland malts tends to remain faithful. Its reputation was built up in the reign of King George IV by word-of-mouth recommendation and unsolicited testimonial, and the fact that its name has been taken as a designation by other malts (the hyphenated Glenlivets) is testimony enough that this product had made its name early in the history of distilling. To discuss its merits is superfluous after so much praise by Professor Sir George Saintsbury and other serious students of wines and spirits.

## TOMATIN

Distilled at Tomatin, Inverness-shire, by Tomatin Distilleries Co. Ltd. An appealing, peaty but light, always likeable single

Highland malt whisky from the go-ahead distillery south of the Highland capital. It is liked by the Invernesians themselves, and they are good judges of genuine malt. The company's trading address is 34 Dover Street, London W1X 4HX.

## TOMINTOUL-GLENLIVET

Distilled at Ballindalloch, Banffshire, by The Tomintoul-Glenlivet Distillery Ltd (a member of The Invergordon Distillers Ltd group). Named after the highest village in the Highlands, this has, like all Highland malts, its own individual appeal (they say there are no two alike, even from closely neighbouring distilleries). Just recently available.

## TORMORE

Distilled at Advie, Speyside, by Long John Distilleries Ltd, 55 Blythswood Street, Glasgow G2 7AT. A pure malt whisky made and matured in the famous area of the Spey valley which has been called "the Golden Rectangle" because most of Scotland's best whiskies are distilled there. It is made with the sparkling water that streams from Loch an Oir (the Lake of Gold) and is named after a neighbouring knoll known in Gaelic as Torr Mór (the Big Hill). The Highland malt whisky produced at this highly modern, efficient and handsome distillery is rich-bodied and delicate to the taste. A splendid 10-year-old Tormore is marketed by Seager Evans & Co. Ltd, 20 Queen Anne's Gate, Westminster, London, S.W.1.

## TULLIBARDINE

Distilled at Blackford, Perthshire, by Tullibardine Distillery Ltd. A Highland malt from near Gleneagles, mellow, mature (10 years old), 80° proof, fine.

## BLENDED OR VATTED MALTS

Several firms bottle vatted malt whiskies—that is to say, selected malt whiskies from various distilleries and even different areas which are blended together and given time to mature further ("marry") in the vat. They are not the same as singles which bear

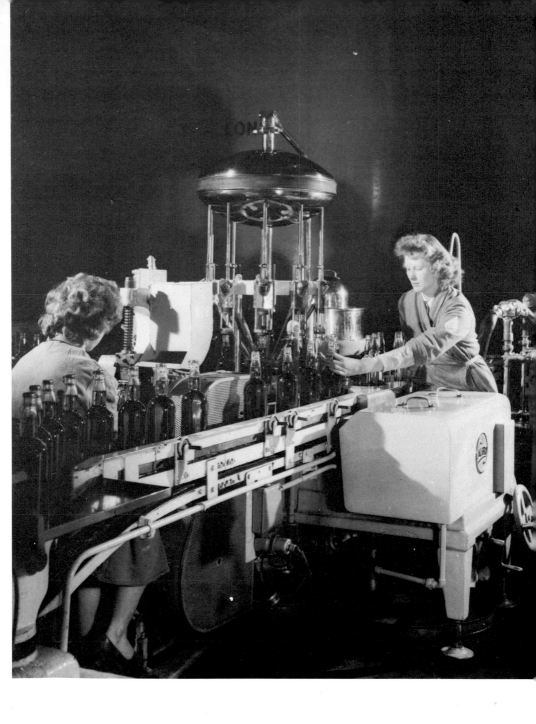

In a blending warehouse of the Distillers Company new bottles are filled (*centre*) by a
rotary machine and inspected (*left*) under a strong light.

In the Talisker stillhouse the resident Excise Officer is seen replacing the padlock on a supply pipe after a new charge of fermented "wash" has been run into a still.

After distillation the spirit has to be at least three years old before it can be sold as "Scotch." During this time it lies in oak casks to mature.

the names of particular distilleries, but they have the merit, for those who prefer pure pot-still whisky to the blends which consist of a good lacing of grain, of being entirely of malt origin. Here are some:

## ALL MALT

Vatted and bottled by Berry Bros & Rudd Ltd, 3 St James's Street, London, S.W.1. These are the blenders of "Cutty Sark," "Berry's Best" and "St James's de Luxe," and the name of such a world-famous firm is sufficient to guarantee the excellence of the choice of malts.

## COCKBURN & MURRAY—THE SEVEN STILLS

Vatted and bottled by Peter J. Russell & Co. Ltd, 45 Frederick Street, Edinburgh EH2 1ET. One hundred per cent malt whisky, 5 years old, from a most reliable Edinburgh blending firm, and with a famous name.

## FINDLATER'S MAR LODGE SCOTCH MALT WHISKY

Vatted and bottled by Findlater (Scotch Whisky) Ltd, 8 Woodside Place, Glasgow. This has the real breath of the heather and is a popular drink with those who favour the barley bree.

## GLEN DRUMMOND

Vatted and bottled by Hankey Bannister & Co. Ltd, 32 Sackville Street, London, W1X 2DA. A grand, strong, true malt whisky from another well-known blender.

## GLEN EAGLE SCOTCH MALT WHISKY

Vatted and bottled by Longman Bonding Co. Ltd, 8 Woodside Place, Glasgow, C.3. A splendid vatting, obtainable 5 years old and 8 years old, by the blenders of "Glen Eagle Scotch Whisky," "Highland Pride" and "Longman de Luxe."

## GLEN LEVEN

Vatted and bottled by John Haig & Co. Ltd, Markinch, Fife. A popular malt from one of the most experienced firms in the making of whiskies to please the palate.

## JULEVEN

Vatted and bottled by Chas H. Julian Ltd, 14 Creechurch Lane, London, E.C.3. This is a sound marriage of compatible Scotch malt whiskies by the blenders of "Excalibur de Luxe."

## JUSTERINI & BROOKS 20 YEARS OLD FINEST MALT

Vatted and bottled by Justerini & Brooks Ltd, 153 New Bond Street, London, W.1. Made mainly for the export market by the blenders of the renowned "J. & B. Rare," this malt whisky is likewise "rare" as a drinking experience.

## STRATHCONON

Vatted and bottled by James Buchanan & Co. Ltd, Devonshire House, Piccadilly, London W1X 6BL. The blenders of "Black & White" and "Buchanan's de Luxe" obviously know what the drinker wants, and this, their contribution to the enjoyment of the malt enthusiasts, shows that the blending skill extends to the mating of good stuff from the pot stills without the interloping grain.

# 6 The Art of the Blender

FROM THE malt distilleries—Highland, Islay, Campbeltown and Lowland—and from the grain distilleries the whiskies come together in the blending houses. Malt may be vatted with malt and grain with grain, but in blending both malt and grain are combined, each blend having its own secret formula, its own discreet proportions and setting of one individual whisky alongside another, and each achieving in its own way that distinctiveness which justifies a label and a name.

There are many famous brands and there are brands too numerous to mention which, although they may not have caught on to the same extent, have found staunch customers here and there. There are about two thousand brands of Scotch whisky. Some may have a local reputation. Some are admired far afield and yet are difficult to obtain except in restricted areas.

What makes a brand distinctive? There may be as many as forty different individual whiskies combined in a particular blend.

They may be malts and grains from quite diverse districts with sharply contrasted flavours or bouquets. The blender assembles them as an artist chooses and mixes his colours, knowing their interaction, their effect one upon another, and knowing how to achieve a pleasing effect quite different from that of any one of the constituents. Upwards of fifteen single whiskies will be in the blend.

The blender has to know which whiskies are incompatible as well as which may wed easily. He must know which gains in quality by juxtaposition with which, which desirable flavour is given more piquancy by contrast with which companion. His aim is not to destroy or delete the constituent whiskies but to enhance them by teaming. He must know when the singles are ready for the match, if they are consistent in themselves and matured to suit his blend, before mixing them together in the blending vat. This involves the detailed testing of innumerable samples, for the blender must make sure of the quality and consistency of every cask.

His guide is not his palate but his nose. He does not taste the samples, he goes by the bouquet, using the tulip glass to guide the aroma to his experienced olfactory nerve.

Only when he is satisfied that the formula is correct and that each constituent is right all through does he consign them to the blending vat, where they are mixed and from which they go once more into cask.

In cask the blend is left for months for the constituents to marry. In some blends the chosen malt whiskies are vatted together and the chosen grain whiskies also are vatted together, the combination of malt and grain being left to near the bottling stage.

While the whiskies lie in casks as individual spirits there is considerable loss in quantity through evaporation. There is loss in gallons also in the process of marrying after blending. So the original output of a distillery reckoned in proof gallons does not represent the ultimate quantity of single or blended whisky available for bottling and despatch.

Age improves the whisky so long as it is in cask, up to fifteen or more years. Once the spirit leaves cask and is bottled, no further change takes place.

Nowadays blending is highly scientific and even computerised. That is the position, for instance, in the big blending and bottling plant of Arthur Bell & Sons Ltd. Substantial stocks of maturing whiskies are held for future blending. Now there is a computerised system of recording these stocks. This makes possible an accurate allocation of mature stock for future blends and ensures that the product is standardised, and the drinker knows from the label that he is getting what he has asked for, a consistent brand.

In such a blending establishment the casks of blended whisky are stored in split-level warehouses. When the marrying process is completed, the whisky is pumped into vats. In these it is reduced with water to bottling strength.

After the oak casks have been emptied they go to the cooperage. There about a thousand casks are inspected and repaired every week before being sent back to the distilleries for refilling.

After being reduced to bottling strength, the whisky is passed through a refrigeration plant. It is then pumped into bottling vats, from which glass pipes carry the spirit to the filling machines at the heads of the bottling lines. Bottling is highly automated nowadays, but there is a strict system of examination of the filled bottles before the conveyor belt takes them on the labelling and packaging machines.

In such vast blending, bottling and despatch complexes as Bell's at East Mains, centuries-old skills, to use their own phrase, are successfully married to modern technology.

From last century, the history of Scotch whisky has been of the successful organisation of blending, bottling, packaging and distribution, and above all of salesmanship, and the story of the men who created and marketed the famous proprietary brands is at least as romantic as that of the old distillers who emerged into legitimate, licensed whisky-making from the caves and hide-outs in the heather and the pony tracks of the smuggling trade.

# 7 The Proprietary Brands

AS IT is easy to be lost in the labyrinth of a couple of thousand brands of Scotch whisky, it is natural to clutch at the well-known names—Bell, Begg, Haig, "Black and White," "White Horse," "Johnnie Walker," "Long John," and the like, most of them names of men who pioneered in blending, starting by catering for Lowlanders in the comparative boom times late last century, when miners and steelworkers were making money and were thirsty for something lighter than pure malt.

If it was the Highlanders who pioneered the distilling of malts it was the Lowlanders who pioneered the patent stills and the blending of whiskies. It began in Edinburgh, and the sea port of the capital, Leith, is still important in the blending and marketing of whisky.

Andrew Usher of Edinburgh was soon followed by other distillers. Some of the most famous blends were started by licensed grocers

who had a shrewd knowledge of what went down with their customers. From early on, good blending went hand in hand with
high-class salesmanship. It was not luck that made such names
as "Johnnie Walker," Grant, Gilbey, "J. & B.," Haig, Begg, Bell,
Dewar and Buchanan famous.

A hundred or more main brands are well-known on the home
market. There are many more exported. There are many brands
known only in certain localities and to limited clienteles.

There is only one criterion affecting your choice of Scotch. Is
it agreeable? Do you like it? Does it like you? In other words,
are you and your whisky compatible?

If you choose an established brand you are sure of consistency.
The label will tell you, along with the quantity in the bottle, the
degree of alcoholic strength. This is usually 70° proof for the home
market and 75° for abroad (70° for Canada and the Common
Market). At the time of filling into casks the distillation is reduced
to 120° proof, which represents 68.7 per cent of alcohol by
volume.

In the process of maturing the strength goes down to perhaps
106° proof (60.5 per cent alcohol) at the age of seven or as low as
100° proof (57.1 per cent alcohol) about twelve years old.

Gin and rum are normally bottled, like whisky, at 70° proof;
sherry, port and madeira at 35° proof (20 per cent alcohol content
by volume), champagne at 23° (13.1 per cent alcohol), Bordeaux
and Burgundy 20° proof (11 per cent) and a strong ginger wine
25° proof (14.2 per cent alcohol). Beer generally is well below 10°
proof.

If an age is given on a label it is the age of the youngest whisky
in the blend. This means that any grain whisky in it, as well as
malt whisky, is at least as old as the label states. Other whiskies
in the same blend may be much, much older.

Several blenders market, in addition to their standard brands,
de luxe brands and brands available only in export markets. There
are many special labels also for export brands, to suit the different
countries in which they sell and even the different agents, and a
large bottling and labelling plant will have a vast variety of labels
to stick on automatically, all to be checked with the utmost care
before despatch.

I have arranged alphabetically a list of de luxe whiskies which
are all worth trying, to find if they suit your palate.

## 100 PIPERS

Blended and bottled by the Glenkeith-Glenlivet Distillery Co. Ltd, Glen Keith Distillery, Keith (Chivas Bros-Seagram-Samuel Bronfman's Distillers Corporation). This is a good Highland type blend which has acquired an appeal to Scotch whisky drinkers even on home territory where the prejudice in favour of some hint of malt is strong. The label is inspired by the old Scots song: "Wi' a hunder pipers an' a', an' a', We'll up and gie them a blaw, a blaw," but the blow from the 100 Pipers in this bottle is a friendly one.

## AMBASSADOR

Blended and bottled in Dumbarton by Taylor & Ferguson Ltd, 3 High Street, a Hiram Walker unit since 1965, distillers of Scapa Highland malt distillery, Kirkwall, Orkney. A stately blend of grains and malts with a well balanced character and some flavour.

## BALLANTINE'S

Blended and bottled by George Ballantine & Sons Ltd, 2 Castle Street, Dumbarton (Hiram Walker). Ballantine's founded Milton-duff-Glenlivet Distillery, Elgin, in 1824, and marketed the famous "Creamy Old Milton Duff Whisky" which spread overseas. Now they operate also the Glencadam Highland malt distillery, Brechin, Angus, taken over by Hiram Walker in 1954. There is a de luxe Ballantine's which has even more of a Highland flavour than the standard. Also two liqueur whiskies—17 years old and 30 years old—for those who like something really special.

## BALLOCHMYLE

Blended and bottled by Watson & Middleton Ltd, 50 Wellington Street, Glasgow G2 6HJ. Scotch whisky blenders do not usually take the name of Robert Burns or any of his creations in vain. They use such labels to convey the warmth and companionship of the Bard. "The bonnie lass o' Ballochmyle" was a damsel the poet longed to press nightly to his bosom, but, short of that, he would have made do with this whisky.

## BEGG'S GOLD CAP

Blended and bottled by John Begg Ltd, Trafalgar House, 75 Hope Street, Glasgow G2 6AJ. Royal Lochnagar was John Begg's distillery. "Take a peg of John Begg" is the company's familiar slogan. This is the de luxe version, which means it has more of Royal Lochnagar, the whisky which charmed Queen Victoria and Prince Albert. John Begg joined DCL in 1916.

**Blue Cap** is Begg's standard blend and not far behind in retaining some of the body and bouquet of the Highland malts while lightening with grain to appeal to the city drinker.

## BELL'S DE LUXE

Blended and bottled in Perth by Arthur Bell & Sons Ltd. A 12-years-old blend of malts and grains with the aura of Dufftown-Glenlivet, Blair Athol and Inchgower. Arthur Bell & Sons Ltd was established in Perth in the year 1825 with a whisky merchant's shop near St John's Kirk purchasing malts from the various distilleries and selling them as singles. It became a pioneering firm in blending and acquired its own three Highland malt distilleries in Buckie, Dufftown and Pitlochry in the 1930s.

**Bell's Royal Vat de Luxe** is a liqueur blended Scotch whisky, mature, mellow and smooth.

**Bell's Extra Special** is the standard drink from Perth to take "Afore Ye Go"—a friendly Doric version of *deoch an doruis* or drink at the door, as the Gaels call a stirrup-cup.

## BENMORE

Blended and bottled by Benmore Distilleries Ltd, 5 Oswald Street, Glasgow G1 4QR, the DCL distillers and blenders who operate the Dallas Dhu Highland malt distillery at Forres, Morayshire. "Fetch ben more!" is a Scottish way of saying: "Same again!" and naming the brand from this or from the great mountain would be equally appropriate.

## BEST PROCURABLE

Blended and bottled by the Hudson's Bay Co. Ltd, 45 Frederick Street, Edinburgh EH2 1YG. A highly selective blend of Scotch grain and malt whiskies, with its own discerning clientele. Edinburgh blenders with their premises in the Georgian New Town have a high reputation among seasoned Scotch whisky drinkers with their own preferences.

## BIG T

Blended and bottled by Tomatin Distillers Co. Ltd, 34 Dover Street, London W1X 4HX. This is a judicious blend from the Highland malt distillers near Inverness, who have a lively sense of the need to keep abreast of the times in equipment, technology and the study of public taste. Their light-bodied peaty malt is popular with other blenders and not neglected in this mature, tasty brand.

## BLACK & WHITE

Blended and bottled by James Buchanan & Co., Devonshire House, Piccadilly, London W1X 6BL, this world-famous brand was originally bottled as *Buchanan* in a black bottle with a white label. It was "the drinking classes" who called it *Black & White* and the astute blender, one of the creators of the world demand for Scotch, exploited their choice of name to the full, even to bringing in the symbol of the black and white Highland terriers ("Real Scotch"). This is a strong favourite in West Germany.

James Buchanan & Co. was founded in 1884 by James Buchanan (later Lord Woolavington), a Scots-Canadian in London. He traded in Scotch whiskies with the help of W. P. Lowrie of Glasgow, then devised his lightened blend for English tastes. He captured the trade in the music halls, theatres and hotels, and even the House of Commons (his brand was labelled *House of Commons* at one stage). Buchanan and Dewar merged in 1915 and in 1925 joined DCL along with John Walker.

There are a delicious **B. & W. De Luxe**, a special **B. & W. Oval** and a mature **B. & W. Twelve**.

Glentauchers and Dalwhinnie Highland malt distilleries come under the Buchanan banner, but there are other good whiskies in de luxe **Buchanan's.**

## BLACK BOTTLE

Blended and bottled by Gordon Graham, Aberdeen (Gordon Graham-Stewart Ltd, Regent House, Regent Quay, Aberdeen). A fine Highland blend of well selected and well matched Scotch malts and Scotch grains, it carries the recommendation of Long John Distilleries Ltd (and so of Schenley Industries Inc of U.S.A.) and is on sale in a number of English hotels, notably the New Forest Hotel near Lyndhurst, Hampshire.

## BLACK SWAN

Blended and bottled by J. & W. Nicholson Ltd, Windsor House, 83 Kingsway, London, W.C.2. A blend of the best, matured and smooth. As well as the historic Black Swan Inn and Black Swan distillery in Holborn, London, there is a Black Swan pub in Edinburgh's Royal Mile marking the spot where Mary Queen of Scots turned on the howling mob which besieged her at a critical stage in her career. If someone had been able to come to her rescue then with a drop of this cratur it would have given her even more courage than she displayed on that critical occasion.

## CAIRNS

Blended and bottled by Eadie Cairns, 11 Bothwell Street, Glasgow G2 6LY. A well-known and widely appreciated blend of contrasted grains and malts by the Auchentoshan Lowland malt distillers of Old Kilpatrick, Dunbartonshire.

There is a good mature brand from the same firm called, with a sense of humour, **B.C.** It is a joke we can take in the spirit in which it is conveyed.

## CHIVAS REGAL

Blended and bottled by Chivas Bros, 111/113 Renfrew Road, Paisley, the original Aberdeen blenders and distillers of Glenkeith-Glenlivet and Strathisla-Glenlivet, both in Keith, Banffshire. Samuel Bronfman himself sponsored the blending of this rich de luxe dram with its medley mainly of mature malts. Chivas Bros became part of Seagrams and the Bronfman empire in 1950.

**Royal Salute.** Another de luxe blend from the same firm and blended with the same attention to the requirements of a good luxury whisky.

**Royal Strathythan.** This is Chivas Bros' standard brand and has a faithful following for its hints of Queen Victoria's beloved Highlands and its pleasant drinking qualities. John Brown would have liked it.

## CHURTONS V.O.B.G.

Blended and bottled by Churtons Ltd, 2 Eberle Street, Liverpool L2 2AH. These North of England enthusiasts for good Scotch whiskies market a variety of worthy brands. The de luxe label is **Churton's VOBG 8 years**, and the Standard brands are **White River, Golden Crest, Buckingham** and **Long Label.**

## CLAN MACLEOD

Blended and bottled by Macleod, Duncan & Co. Ltd, 242 Clyde Street, Glasgow G2 4JH. A de luxe blend of well selected grains and malts taking care of the malt flavour.

**Old Crofter.** The standard brand from this wise blending firm, with a taste of the mellow malt of the crofter counties coming through.

## CLUNY

Blended and bottled in Leith, "the whisky capital of Scotland," by John E. McPherson & Sons Ltd, 111 Holyrood Road, Edinburgh EH8 8AY. The address is that of administrative offices of Scottish & Newcastle Breweries Ltd, formed in 1960 of Scottish Brewers (William Younger and William McEwan of Edinburgh) and Newcastle Breweries, who took over the McPherson firm in 1952. This is a light whisky with a good overseas clientele. **Cluny de Luxe** is 12 years old.

## COCKBURN & MURRAY

Blended and bottled by Peter J. Russell & Co. Ltd, 45 Frederick Street, Edinburgh EH2 1ET. Another famous Edinburgh New Town blend. There are an excellent 4 years old and a de luxe 8 years old. From the same blending house come two favourites, **Black Rooster** and **Black Shield.**

## CRABBIE

Bottled and blended by John Crabbie & Co. Ltd, 108 Great Junction Street, Leith, Edinburgh EH6 5LF. John Crabbie & Co. were among the pioneer distilling firms and users of patent still grain whisky who formed a trading agreement in 1856 and they are now part of DCL. They are distillers of Balmenach-Glenlivet Highland malt distillery in Cromdale and famous for their green ginger wine which is a favourite concomitant with whisky in Scotland at Hogmanay.

**Crabbie's Special Reserve 12 Years Old** is a de luxe blend with a Speyside emphasis and **Crabbie 8 Years Old** is another smooth drinking and tasteful blend.

## CRAWFORD FIVE STAR

Blended and bottled by A. & A. Crawford, 93 Constitution Street, Leith, Edinburgh EH6 7AN. Archibald and Aikman Crawford were two brothers who started their business in Leith in 1860. The family company became part of DCL in 1944, but the seventy-year-old "Three Star" label was naturally kept on. It is a great favourite in Edinburgh. The de luxe "Five Star" was added after the Great War in the party-throwing twenties, and quickly caught on. You will find Crawford's "stars" (three or five according to the state of the pocket) in many Edinburgh drinkers' eyes and the appeal goes far beyond the Scottish capital. **Crawford's Special Reserve** is much liked.

## CUTTY SARK

Blended and bottled in Scotland by Berry Bros & Rudd Ltd, 3 St James's St, London, S.W.1. Distributed in the United Kingdom by Cutty Sark (U.K. Scotch Whisky) Ltd, 106 West Nile Street, Glasgow, C.1. Its "million dollar" name has a double significance for Scotch drinkers, as well as the famous windjammer or clipper sailing craft depicted on the label (and the whisky has gone round the world as conspicuously as the ship), "Cutty Sark" was the nickname of the short-shirted young witch who stole away the senses of Robert Burns's "Tam o' Shanter" that wild night at Kirk Alloway on his whisky-inspired ride from Ayr to Brig o' Doon. The firm started in 1803 as Berry Bros and Hugh Rudd joined in 1920, adding his name to the company formed in 1940. Schenley Industries Inc. control the Buckingham Corporation which puts over this strong light blend which was supposed to take a trick when it strayed into the States in Prohibition times. At 70° or 75° proof it can be taken neat and has been compared to brandy.

"Cutty Sark" boasts it is "Double barreled" because after being blended it is casked once more to lie for 18 months to marry, mellow and mature further, a secret of good blending.

**Berry's Best** is a de luxe from the "Cutty Sark" blenders.

**St James's** is another famous one.

## DANDIE DINMONT

Blended and bottled by A. Alexander & Co. Ltd, 111 Holyrood Road, Edinburgh EH8 8AY. There are both standard and export brands of this popular blend from one of the firms now under the banner of Scottish & Newcastle Breweries Ltd. The name is taken from an "honest" character in the *Waverley Novels*. In whisky nomenclature a good Scottish name is attractive, but it has to be backed by real Scotch behind the label.

## DAVID ROSS'S DE LUXE

Blended and bottled by Campbell & Clark Ltd, 35 Robertson Street, Glasgow G2 8HE. A blend of grains and malts which retains the Highland character.

**Clark's Reserve** is the firm's standard, soothing and tasteful, and there are sterling qualities in the firm's **Duncan's Reserve, Campbell's Private Stock** and **Tranquility.**

## FINDLATER'S FINEST OLD

Blended and bottled by Findlater (Scotch Whisky) Ltd, 8 Woodside Place, Glasgow C.3. A good grain and malt Scotch whisky blend by the vatters of Mar Lodge Scotch malt whisky, a firm with a sound grasp of what pleases and satisfies the drinker of the traditional Highland product.

## FOUR CROWN

Blended and bottled by Seagram Distillers Ltd, 111/113 Renfrew Road, Paisley. Samuel Bronfman took over Joseph Seagram & Sons as a step towards his multi-million-pound Distillers Corporation in Canada in 1928. Seagrams was a Canadian whisky distilling firm. They took over Milton, Keith (Strathisla-Glenlivet), and added Glen Keith distillery, Keith Maltings and Keith Bonds, bringing in Chivas Bros of Aberdeen. Now they have a huge blending and bottling complex in Paisley and Dalmuir. This is one of their good blends of well chosen whiskies.

## GAUNTLET

Blended and bottled by James Sword & Son Ltd, 102 Holm Street, Glasgow, C.2. A good mature blend with more than a local reputation in which good grain goes hand in glove with sturdy malt.

**Bank Note** is James Sword's much appreciated de luxe. Whatever may happen to "the pound in your pocket," you can rely on the quality of the bottle in your pocket staying the same.

## GILT EDGE

Blended and bottled by McGown & Cameron Ltd, 2360 Dumbarton Road, Glasgow, W.4. A sumptuous blend of rich malts lightened by well selected grain.

## GLEN EAGLE SCOTCH WHISKY

Blended and bottled in Glasgow by Longman Bonding Co. Ltd, 8 Woodside Place. An 8 years old de luxe with a pleasant Highland character and smooth drinking consistency. There is a standard brand.

**Longman de Luxe** is another rich blend from this company. Also worth sampling: **Highland Pride Scotch Whisky.**

## GLENFINNAN ROYAL LIQUEUR

Blended and bottled by David Sandeman & Sons Ltd, 242 Clyde Street, Glasgow G1 4JH. The de luxe brand of this reliable blending firm, whose standard brands, **Glenfinnan** and **King's Vat**, also command a good place in the market.

## GLEN GHOIL

Blended and bottled by Hall & Bramley Ltd, National Bank Building, Liverpool L2 7NG. A de luxe brand with a Highland character. Glen Ghoil (*Gleann Goill*) is Gaelic for the valley of the Saxon or stranger, and the blend of true Scotch whiskies by a North of England firm beckons the visitor to the Highlands where the best whiskies originate.

## GLEN ROSSIE SPECIAL RESERVE

Blended and bottled by Glen Rossie Distillers Ltd, 85/89 Duke Street, Liverpool, 1. A blend of Scotch grain and malt whiskies from various parts of Scotland, with the true Highland appeal. Two other good brands from the same house: **Glen Rossie Anniversary** and **Glen Rossie Liqueur.**

## GOLD LABEL

Blended and bottled by John & Robert Harvey Ltd, 5 Oswald Street, Glasgow G1 4QR, distillers of Aultmore-Glenlivet, Keith, on licence from Scottish Malt Distillers Ltd (DCL). This is a grand de luxe.

**Harvey's Special.** The standard brand, also made for the palate of the drinker who welcomes the lightness of grain whiskies but wants to taste the character of good malts. Consistency also is an essential merit: the drinker knows what he is ordering.

## HAIG DIMPLE

Blended and bottled by John Haig & Co. Ltd, Markinch, Fife. Delicious, lingering in flavour. "Don't be vague, Ask for Haig," to which might be added: "Make it simple: Ask for Dimple." Called after its characteristic bottle, a shrewd marketing device which the firm wisely protects, this de luxe blended whisky is a winner in many parts of the world and as much appreciated at home.

The Haigs are a highly placed Border family whose most famous member was a Great War field-marshal, born in Edinburgh. Robert Haig was distilling whisky at Throsk, Stirlingshire, in 1623. Three Haig family firms had distilleries in the Lowlands making patent still whisky last century and went into the English market. John Haig of Cameron Bridge Distillery, Fife, was one of the six founders of DCL in 1877. Haig & Haig were acquired by DCL in 1919 and John Haig & Co. (appointed purveyors to the House of Lords in 1906) merged with DCL in 1924. "The oldest name in distilling" is a fair claim.

Standard brands: **Haig; Gold Label.**

## HANKEY BANNISTER

Blended and bottled by Hankey Bannister & Co. Ltd, 32 Sackville Street, London, W1X 2DA. A well-known and widely welcomed blend of mature malts and good grains from various parts of Scotland. The name of the blending firm is a sufficient guarantee of reliability for them to proclaim it proudly as the title of the blend.

Coleburn Distillery, Longmorn, Morayshire, one of over forty malt distilleries owned by DCL.

Drying malt over a fire in which peat is burned imparts a characteristic flavour and aroma which later passes into the whisky. (White Horse photograph).

The finished product. Some 500 girls operate the bottling lines at the Johnnie Walker plant, Kilmarnock. Separate machines fill, fit screw-tops and stick labels. To avoid monotony and to maintain a meticulously high standard the girls change jobs every half hour.

A warehouseman using "valinche" draws a sample from every cask for examination by the White Horse blender.

## HARRODS

Blended and bottled by Harrods Limited, Knightsbridge, London, SW1. A de luxe blend available in the United Kingdom exclusively through Harrods and House of Fraser Stores. It is produced for Harrods by Whyte & Mackay Ltd, the marketing company in the Dalmore, Whyte & Mackay Group which was taken over by Scottish & Universal Investments in April 1972. The chairman of Scottish & Universal Investments is Sir Hugh Fraser, and the company have approximately a 25 per cent interest in the House of Fraser.

About twenty different malts, including Speysides, Highlands, Lowlands and Islands whiskies are used in the blend. The full flavour of a malt Scotch whisky predominates but the taste is smoother and mellower and the blend is light enough in body for the city drinker and for any time of the day.

Harrods also have their label on **V.O.H.** and **Speyside** pure malt blend.

## HEATHER DEW

Blended and bottled by Mitchell Bros Ltd, 5 Oswald Street, Glasgow G1 4QR, the DCL distillers and blenders who operate North Port Highland malt distillery, Brechin, Angus. There is the breath of the heather-clad slopes and the sparkle of pure mountain water sustaining the liveliness and richness of the carefully selected and knowledgably intermingled grains and malts of varied Scotch origin.

## HIGHLAND CLAN

Blended and bottled by The Highland Bonding Co. Ltd, 111/113 Renfrew Road, Paisley. This is another company belonging to the Chivas Bros Ltd-Seagram Distillers-Distillers Corporation combine, with its links with Canada and the United States. The Paisley blending and bottling plant with its Dalmuir warehouse and other extensions turns out some of the best-known modern whisky brands. There is an old Scottish saying: "Keep your eye on Paisley!" and with American and Canadian enterprise taking a hand in the marketing of Scotch distilled, blended and bottled whiskies, the phrase takes on more significance. Paisley used to be singled out for one of Scotland's model towns with a variety of industries, and whisky blending is now one of the most important. This blend has more than a hint of Highland malt.

## HIGHLAND CREAM

Blended and bottled by William Teacher & Sons Ltd, 14 St Enoch Square, Glasgow C.1. The firm was founded by a go-ahead 19-years-old retailer of spirits, William Teacher, in 1830 and now has Ardmore, Kennethmont, and Glendronach, Aberdeenshire, Highland malt distilleries, as well as an interest in glass art objects and bottle manufacture. A justly renowned brand, much liked in Scotland, peaty, sweet, with that rich creamy quality associated with mature Highland malts but by virtue of the grain, light enough for the more delicate city drinker.

## HIGHLAND MONARCH

Blended and bottled by James Boyle & Co. Ltd, 127 St Vincent Street, Glasgow G2 5JF. A blend of grains and malts which retains the "Monarch of the Glen" Highland aura. "The stag at eve had drunk its fill," but the stag party is not over so long as there is a drop in this bottle.

## HIGHLAND QUEEN

Blended and bottled by Macdonald & Muir Ltd, Queen's Dock, Leith, Edinburgh EH6 6NN. The standard brand is 4 years old. This 80-years-old company have Glenmorangie, Tain, and Glen Moray, Elgin, Highland malt distilleries, and their Glenmorangie is among the top Highland malt single whiskies. "Highland Queen" has built up a reputation as a pleasant blend with a North of Scotland accent. The queen in the advertisements is apparently Mary Queen of Scots looking her best, but the brand has a happier reign than the monarch it commemorates. If only John Knox could have tasted this, perhaps things in Mary's Scotland might have been more peaceful and amicable.

For superior quality you have a choice of **Highland Queen Grand 10, Highland Queen Grand 15** and **Highland Queen Grand Liqueur.**

## HOLT'S BUFF LABEL

Blended and bottled by Stanley Hold & Son Ltd, 1780 London Road, Glasgow E.2. The firm is represented also in Manchester 20. This is an established blend of well chosen and balanced Scotch grains and Scotch malt whiskies, passed by sound judges of a good dram in the Second City.

## ISLAY MIST

Blended and bottled by D. Johnston & Co. (Laphroaig) Ltd, Port Ellen, Islay. Long John Distilleries Ltd claim that this de luxe with its emphasis on the peaty malt of the Inner Hebridean isle is "the unique blend," and it is certainly out on its own as a delectable Scotch drink. The distillers further say it has the cachet and exclusiveness of a chateau-bottled wine. "No other blended whisky is quite like it: a subdued mingling of 8-year-old grain, Speyside and Islay whiskies. Smooth, subtle, mellow." To be sipped neat. It is obtainable also as **Islay Mist 8 y.o.** from Seager Evans & Co. Ltd, 20 Queen Anne's Gate, Westminster, London S.W.1.

## J. & B. RARE

Blended and bottled at Strathleven by Justerini & Brooks Ltd, 61 St James's Street, London S.W.1. Giacomo Justerini, an 18th century Italian immigrant, started this London wine merchants firm in 1749, Mr Brooks taking over in 1831. Now the firm is part of International Distillers and Vintners (which embraces W. & A. Gilbey and the Peter Dominic retail chain, as well as being associated with the Watney Mann brewery combine). J. & B. are probably the best known initials in whisky blending, internationally and especially in the United States. There are strong Speyside Highland malt connections.

**Royal Ages** (15 years old) is a Justerini & Brooks de luxe with an eye on the export trade.

## JOHNNIE WALKER

Blended and bottled in Kilmarnock, Ayrshire, by John Walker & Sons. The original John Walker, who looked, they say, very like the striding dandy in Tom Brown's "Born 1820, still going strong" poster, was a grocer, wine and spirit merchant, in the Ayrshire town. His Glasgow-trained son, Alexander Walker, who joined the firm in 1857, opened offices in London and went all out for the English trade. It was very much a family firm when it became John Walker & Sons Ltd in 1886 (there were grandchildren in it also) and soon afterwards it was the biggest firm of Scotch whisky blenders and exporters in the world. They took over Cardow and other Highland malt distilleries. As one of the Scotch whisky Big Five, Walker in 1925 joined DCL with the already merged Buchanan and Dewar.

**Black Label.** This de luxe caught on and more or less sold itself by its sheer excellence and is still one of the best, most reliable blends.

**Red Label** is the standard Johnnie Walker and has its staunch adherents appreciative of its strength, palatability and maturity.

## JOHNNY WRIGHT'S

Blended and bottled by Reid, Wright & Holloway (Distillers) Ltd, Windsor House, 83 Kingsway, London, W.C.2. When it comes to choosing the right malts to go together and the right grains to make the blend suitable for not so narrowly Caledonian tastes, and wedding the grain with malt in cask to mature that little longer together and "get to know one another," you can't go wrong with Johnny Wright.

## JULIAN'S FINEST

Blended and bottled by Chas H. Julian Ltd, 14 Creechurch Lane, London, E.C.3. The firm has Highland malt distilleries at Knockando and Strathmill, Keith, and the character of good malt is far from absent in this sensitive blend.

**Excalibur** is Julian's de luxe, a well conceived blend of Scotch grain and Scotch malts. They also have **Monument** and **Camlan.**

## KING GEORGE IV

Blended and bottled at South Queensferry by The Distillers Agency Ltd, 7 Coates Crescent, Edinburgh EH3 7AB. The name was registered in 1903 when the new blending and bottling warehouse was built near the Forth Railway Bridge (now accompanied by the Forth Road Bridge) by DCL. The label shows King George IV as he appeared in Edinburgh on his State Visit in 1822, when he expressed such interest in Scotch whisky. The brand has become popular with Lowland Scots.

**King George IV Supreme** is a de luxe blend of selected grain and malt whiskies and also a favourite even on its native heath, a good test of Scotch, as we are often highly critical of what is produced next door to ourselves.

## KING'S RANSOM

Blended and bottled by Wm Whiteley & Co., Atlas House, 57a Catherine Place, Westminster, London, S.W.1, the distillers of Edradour, Pitlochry. A de luxe brand with the Highland malts well represented, not to be missed for a King's ransom. William Whiteley is a Leith name in blending from Victorian and Edwardian times and their distillery is noted for its tiny quaint character as well as its good blending malt. "King's Ransom" is available at 82.5° proof.

## LANG'S

Blended and bottled by Lang Bros Ltd, 10 Oswald Street, Glasgow, the distillers of Glengoyne Highland malt distillery, Killearn, Stirlingshire. A pleasant standard brand with malt overtones. This is a Robertson & Baxter Ltd (The Highland Distilleries Company Ltd) associate. There is an excellent mature blend much in demand by experienced Scotch whisky drinkers—**Lang's 12 Year Old de Luxe.**

## LAUDER'S

Blended and bottled by Archibald Lauder & Co. Ltd, 3 High Street, Dumbarton. This is a Hiram Walker firm and a grand old name in Scotch whisky blending. Not surprisingly the brand is an old favourite.

## LIQUEUR CREAM

Blended and bottled by Saccone & Speed Ltd, 22 Sackville Street, London W1X 2DA. This is another well-known and well-esteemed London name in Scotch whisky blending, and this liqueur Scotch whisky has many devotees.

## LONG JOHN

Blended and bottled by Long John Distilleries Ltd, 55 Blythswood Street, Glasgow G2 7AT. A grand blend named after Long John Macdonald or Macdonell of Keppoch who built Ben Nevis distillery and produced "Long John's Dew of Ben Nevis." He would appreciate this modern blend with a Highland accent which was developed by W. H. Chaplin & Co. Ltd of London. Long John Distilleries at Strathclyde, Tormore, Kinclaith and Glenugie were taken over in 1935 by Seager Evans, which in 1956 became a subsidiary of Schenley Industries Inc. of U.S.A. Laphroaig (Islay) and Tormore (Highland) are two of the great malt whiskies which combine with the matured, gentle grain to give Long John its distinction of flavour and bouquet.

**Long John 8 year old**, the mature de luxe, is available from Seager Evans & Co. Ltd, Queen Anne's Gate, Westminster, London SW1 H9AA. Also **Long John 12 year old**, and **Long John de Luxe**, aged in once-used sherry casks for that while longer which makes it deliciously soft and mellow.

## McCALLUM'S PERFECTION

Blended and bottled by D. & J. McCallum Ltd, 4 Picardy Place, Edinburgh EH1 3JZ, the firm (now DCL) which operates Highland malt distilleries at Cragganmore, Ballindalloch, Banffshire, and Glenlochy, Fort William, and has its administrative offices in what was once the Flemish weaving village of Picardy in Edinburgh, directly opposite the birthplace of Sir Arthur Conan Doyle, the creator of Sherlock Holmes (Doyle's birthplace has been demolished recently along with one side of Picardy Place and part of Union Place, now represented by a traffic roundabout). This is one of my favourite blends because, although not a pure malt, it has that touch about it.

**McCallum's de Luxe.** A much-loved high-class blend. It was for their customers of the Tattie-Pit pub in Edinburgh over a hundred years ago that the McCallums blended this peaty dram.

## MACGREGOR'S

Blended and bottled by MacGregor & Ross Ltd, 50 Wellington Street, Glasgow G2 6HJ. A charming blend of judiciously chosen Scotch whiskies, bland but tasty.

**Scottish Heath.** ("My foot is on my native heath, and my name's MacGregor.") A companion blend with its own clan of faithful followers.

## MACKINLAY'S LEGACY

Blended and bottled in Leith by Charles Mackinlay & Co. Ltd, 111 Holyrood Road, Edinburgh EH8 8AY. The address here is the Scottish & Newcastle Breweries Ltd one near Holyrood Palace, but the Mackinlay-McPherson blending house is in Salamander Place near Leith Links, and is the source of brands which go to all parts of the world. Mackinlays was established in 1815 (James Buchanan was their agent in London in 1879) and it is still run by the same family, though part of Scottish & Newcastle Breweries since 1961. The company is associated with the Isle of Jura Distillery Co. Ltd and Glenallachy Distillery, Aberlour, Banffshire, built in 1968, and looks after whisky distilling, blending, marketing and other wine and spirits interests of the breweries combine (see the note on McPherson's "Cluny" brand). The "Legacy" is a mature and mellow blend of well selected grain and malt whiskies from a most experienced company of blenders. Until recently McKinlay & Birnie, another associate company, exported Glen Mohr and Glen Albyn Highland malts, but these distilleries have been acquired mainly for blending by DCL. Charles Mackinlay's have just launched a new Isle of Jura malt (see Chapter 5).

## MACLEAY DUFF

Blended and bottled by Macleay Duff (Distillers) Ltd, 5 Oswald Street, Glasgow G1 4QR. A good standard blend with a solid reputation by an established blending firm now part of DCL.

**Macleay Duff Antique Extra Special.** The de luxe version, mature, mellow, matey.

**Macleay Duff Special Matured Cream** if you believe in pampering yourself.

## MACNISH V.L.

Blended and bottled by Robert Macnish & Co. Ltd, 2 Glasgow Road, Dumbarton. This is one of two standard brands which have caught on from this Hiram Walker firm, the other being **Doctor's Special.**

**Grand Macnish** is a de luxe blend of a wide range of mature Scotch whiskies, grain and malt.

## MAK' READIE

Blended and bottled by James McCreadie & Co. Ltd, 106 West Nile Street, Glasgow. A de luxe blend of mature grain with mellow malts, achieving mildness without sacrifice of strength of character. Also from Reid, Stuart & Co. Ltd, London, S.E.8.

## M.D. GOLDEN CROWN

Blended and bottled in Leith by Melrose-Drover Ltd, 17 Mitchell Street, Leith, Edinburgh EH6 7BE. A distinctive blend from the "whisky capital of Scotland," the seaport of the Scottish capital. Also **M.D. Doctor Label** and **M.D. Ancient & Honourable**, a smooth, mature, suave, sophisticated de luxe.

## MURRAY BURN

Blended and bottled by Tullibardine Distillery Ltd, 183 Pitt Street, Glasgow C.2. The distillery on which it is based is at Blackford in Perthshire, and the name commemorates the Murrays of Perthshire as well as the interest of R. Murray (Rutland Investment Trust Ltd), Bonnyrigg. The blend contrives to preserve the appeal of good Highland malt whisky discreetly modified by other malts and Scotch grain whiskies.

## NAVY SUPREME

Blended and bottled by John Hopkins & Co. Ltd, 5 Oswald Street, Glasgow G1 4QR, the DCL company which operates the St Magdalene Lowland malt distillery at Linlithgow, the town where Mary Queen of Scots was born. The de luxe brand with its slight brandy touch from the Lowland malt would not shame the Fleet. Hopkins have two standard brands with a Highland slant—**Glen Garry** and **Old Mull**

## NORTHERN SCOT

Blended and bottled by Bruce & Co. (Leith) Ltd, 111 Holyrood Road, Edinburgh EH8 8AY. Again a brand from Scottish & Newcastle Breweries Ltd. The Newcastle breweries were interested in whisky blending when they took over the old Newcastle Scotch blending firm of John E. McPherson in 1952. The Edinburgh brewing firms of William Younger (1749) and William McEwan (1856) combined to form Scottish Brewers in 1931 and joined up with Newcastle breweries in 1960, purchasing Charles Mackinlay's in 1961 and forming the Mackinlay-McPherson distilling and blending branch based on two old and distinguished firms from Leith and Newcastle-on-Tyne. This is another brand with a North Country appeal.

## OLD COURT

Blended and bottled by A. Gillies & Co. (Distillers) Ltd, 140 Renfield Street, Glasgow C.2, who since 1955 have operated the old Scotia (now Glen Scotia) Campbeltown malt distillery. The title of this good blend made for both the home and export trade recalls the Royal Court of King Fergus of the Scots away back in the 6th century, and of course emphasises the maturity and courtly charm of the brand. They have another with sterling qualities called **Royal Escort**, again blended for export.

## OLD CURIO

Blended and bottled by Peter Dawson, Trafalgar House, 75 Hope Street, Glasgow G2 6AP, the DCL firm which operates Ord distillery in Wester Ross. At 76° proof this mature de luxe blend has a grand flavour and bouquet and is very pleasant to drink. It is rivalled from the same stable by **Rare Reserve** also at 76° proof, and the firm's standard brand, **Peter Dawson Special**, is keenly sought by Scotch whisky enthusiasts.

## OLD RARITY

Blended and bottled by Bulloch Lade Ltd, 75 Hope Street, Glasgow G2 6AW, the famous DCL blenders who operate Caol Ila (Strait of Islay) malt distillery at Port Askaig. The firm was originally Bulloch & Co., owners of Loch Katrine Distillery and Lossit Islay malt distillery. About the middle of last century they combined with Lade & Co. and shortly afterwards purchased Caol Ila. This 75° proof mature de luxe blend is light but with the piquancy of the island peat reek in its friendly approach, and is consequently drunk with great appreciation.

**B.L. Gold Label** is the well-known standard brand and a very happy blend of mature grains and malts, while there are two much admired aristocrats from the same house, **King Arthur** and **Marlboro.**

## OLD SMUGGLER

Blended and bottled by James & George Stodart Ltd, 3 High Street, Dumbarton, the Hiram Walker distillers and blenders who operate Glenburgie-Glenlivet Highland malt distillery at Forres, exporting Glenburgie-Glenlivet and marketing also the other popular Highland malt single, Old Pulteney. A grand malty blend.

## PERTH ROYAL

Blended and bottled by Matthew Gloag & Son Ltd, Bordeaux House, Kinnoull Street, Perth. The firm goes back to 1814 and was bought by Highland Distilleries in 1970. This de luxe blend has the strong appeal of the mountains and glens along with the mature civilised approach of the ancient capital of Scotland and gateway to the North.

**Famous Grouse Brand** is the delightful standard Gloag blend with an appeal to the Twelfth of August sports and to all drinkers of friendly Scotch, sweet with a hint of peat and rich old malt.

## PIGEON BLEND

Blended and bottled in Glasgow by Samuel Dow Ltd, 242 Clyde Street G1 4JH, one of the Second City firms with a long standing reputation for catering for their customers' known tastes. This has all the strength of real Scotch whisky and its smack of the heather and peat but "will roar you as gently as a sucking dove."

## P.T. OLD PERTH LIQUEUR

Blended and bottled by Peter Thomson (Perth) Ltd, P.O. Box 22, King Edward Street, Perth. This established firm of the old Scottish Court city is one that deals in malt whiskies as well as in well balanced and mature blends, and this is a heart-warming de luxe blend of some of the best of them. The firm's standard brand is **Beneagles**, with the tang of the Perthshire forests.

## QUEEN'S OWN

Blended and bottled by Grants of St James' Ltd, 87 Station Street, Burton-on-Trent. A substantial, subtle and sustaining blend available on the home and overseas markets.

## RED HACKLE

Blended and bottled by Hepburn & Ross Ltd, Kelvin House, 19/39 Otago Street, Kelvinbridge, Glasgow G12 8JJ, named from the favour displayed in the headgear of the oldest Highland Regiment, the Black Watch, has a staunch following both in the Second City and around the world. It is marketed by Robertson & Baxter Ltd for the Highland Distilleries Co. Ltd. **Red Hackle de Luxe** is a mature and smooth-drinking blend of highly selected grains and malts.

## RED TAPE

Blended and bottled by Baird-Taylor Ltd, Trafalgar House, 75 Hope Street, Glasgow G2 6AJ. An established blend from a firm now part of DCL, who have another good brand called Baird's.

## ROBBIE BURNS

Blended and bottled by R. H. Thomson & Co. (Distillers) Ltd, 5 Maritime Street, Leith, Edinburgh EH6 6SB, a DCL company and distillers of Teaninich, Easter Ross. This is a heartsome dram which is worthy of the name of the man who wrote: "Freedom and whisky gang thegither."

**Old Angus** is another good blend from Thomson's of Leith. Angus in Gaelic myth was the spirit of youth and this blend proves the paradox that the older Scotch whisky becomes in the cask, the younger it makes you feel.

## ROYAL EDINBURGH

Blended and bottled by Ainslie & Heilbron (Distillers) Ltd, 5 Oswald Street, Glasgow G1 4QU. This DCL distilling and blending firm has the famous Clynelish Highland malt distillery in Brora, Sutherland, and this is a widely appreciated blend of compatible mature grains and malts.

**Specially Selected** is their de luxe brand, a blend which has won many adherents by its rich flavour and pleasant smoothness.

## ROYAL MILE

Blended and bottled by George Morton Ltd, Dundee. A de luxe blend made with attention to maturity and appeal to the discerning palate.

**Morton's Blended.** An attractive standard brand from the same experienced blending firm, with some character and easy to drink.

## SANDEMAN

Blended and bottled by G. Sandeman Sons & Co. Ltd, 37 Albert Embankment, London S.E.1. A well balanced combination of mature grains and old malts with an appeal to the clubman.

## SANDEMAN'S V.V.O.

Blended and bottled by Sandeman & Sons Ltd, Edinburgh. A de luxe blend of "very very old" whiskies by a firm well established in the wine and spirits trade and experienced blenders of Scotch for the fastidious drinker.

**The King of Whiskies**, the firm's standard brand, has wide acceptability for its tastefulness and mellow smoothness.

## SANDY MACDONALD

Blended and bottled by Macdonald Greenlees Ltd, 5 Maritime Street, Leith, Edinburgh EH6 6SF, a tried and trusty blending house in the DCL group. This is their standard brand and much favoured by true Scots. The firm operates the Speyside Highland malt distillery of Glendullan, Dufftown.

**Old Parr** and **President** are two pleasing, mature de luxe brands, and **Claymore** is another standard brand with a Highland flourish, this being the English spelling of the Gaelic *claidheamh mór* (great sword), the weapon of fighting Scots in the brave days long ago.

## SANDY TAMSON

Blended and bottled by The Glenfyne Distillery Co. Ltd, 106 West Nile Street, Glasgow, C.1. A judicious blend, mellow, strong, pleasant. This company distils at Ardrishaig Highland malt distillery, Argyll.

## SCOTTISH CREAM

Blended and bottled by The Kinloch Distillery Co. Ltd, 106 West Nile Street, Glasgow C.1. A mature, mellow and tasteful blend that has caught on in the export trade, handled by Robertson Baxter Ltd (The Highland Distilleries Co. Ltd).

## SCOTTISH HIGHLAND

Blended and bottled by James Catto & Co. Ltd, 1 York Gate, Regent's Park, London N.W.1. The company is in the Gilbey's (International Distillers & Vintners) group. This is a rich, 12-years-old blend combining the character of good Highland malt with the discretion of very mature grain whisky.

**Rare Old Scottish Highlands** and **Gold Label** are two other distinguished brands with the Catto imprint.

## SOMETHING SPECIAL

Blended and bottled by Hill, Thomson & Co. Ltd, Frederick Street, Edinburgh. This famous concern was started in Rose Street Lane in the Scottish capital's New Town in 1793. A particularly good de luxe blend of mutually stimulating Scotch grains and malts from this grand old firm, whose famous standard brand, **Queen Anne**, has a grand Speyside flavour and whose **St Leger** is also a delight to drink. Since 1970 the firm has been part of the Glen Grant-Glenlivet group.

## SPEY-ROYAL

Blended and bottled by W. & A. Gilbey Ltd, 1 York Gate, Regent's Park, London N.W.1, who have their Highland malt distilleries at Knockando, Glen Spey, Rothes, and Strathmill, Keith. The Speyside flavour is unmistakeable in this grand blend. Gilbey's are important in the International Distillers & Vintners combine, associated also with the Bass Charrington brewery chain, but their history goes back to the middle of last century when they were Continental wine importers. Before the end of the century they went into malt whisky distilling and developed their blending.

## STANDFAST

Blended and bottled by Wm Grant & Sons Ltd, 206/208 West George Street, Glasgow G2 2LW. William Grant was a Dufftown man who learned his trade at Mortlach Distillery (then Gordon & Cowie's) and bought Cardow for £120 to build his own distillery in 1886, also founding one of the most famous and most effective families in both distilling and blending. This is a deservedly popular blend of good grain and various well selected malt whiskies and its command of the home market has recently greatly increased. The firm has Glenfiddich, Balvenie, Girvan and Ladybank distilleries.

**Best Procurable**, a choice de luxe blend by this highly reputable firm.

## STEWART'S DUNDEE DE LUXE

Blended and bottled by Stewart & Son of Dundee Ltd, Stewart House, Kingsway East, Dundee. A de luxe whisky of good taste, strength and maturity by blenders of initiative and experience.

**Cream of the Barley.** A likeable blend of many whiskies with the accent on malt, much in demand.

## TALISMAN

Blended and bottled by Lambert Bros (Edinburgh) Ltd, 9/11 Frederick Street, Edinburgh EH2 2EY. A well selected and judiciously balanced blend, mainly for export.

**The Monarch.** Lambert Bros' de luxe brand, a majestic blend of mutually compatible grains and malts, delicious and gentle.

## THE ABBOT'S CHOICE

Blended and bottled by Low Robertson & Co. Ltd (John McEwan & Co. Ltd), 10 Links Place, Leith, Edinburgh EH6 7HA. John McEwan's original blend. There is no record of who the abbot was, but for a pillar of the church he was a sound judge. This old-established firm, now part of the DCL group, are distillers of Port Ellen, Islay. Linkwood whisky, however, plays an important part in this blend, which is widely famed for its excellence and combines the virtues of a grand selection of mature Scotch whiskies of all types.

**Chequers de Luxe** is a special brand from the same firm and is in many a connoisseur's cellar. The other blends, worth having, are **Ben Calley, Dormy, Grey Label** and **Loretto**.

## THE ANTIQUARY

Blended and bottled by J. & W. Hardie, 27 The Loan, South Queensferry, West Lothian, made within sight of the two great bridges over the Rover Forth by a firm which has been part of DCL since 1947 and operates the Benromach-Glenlivet Highland malt distillery. This is one of the de luxe blends most highly esteemed by dedicated Scotch whisky drinkers in the land of its origin and abroad. It has the lightness and gentleness of mature grain and the richness and character of good malts.

## THE HIELANMAN

Blended and bottled by Wm Cadenhead, 47 Netherkirkgate, Aberdeen. A heartsome dram with a distinctive Highland flavour, by dealers in malt whisky who do not neglect the real MacKay in their blends.

**Putachieside de Luxe** is the de luxe blend from this distinguished North Country house and a collector's bottle.

## THISTLE BLEND

Blended and bottled by Slater, Roger & Co. Ltd, 401 Scotland Street, Glasgow G41 1LD. They operate Banff Highland malt distillery and are part of DCL, and this is a worthy Scotch blend.

**Roger's Old Scots** is another more than acceptable blend from this same grand old Glasgow blending firm.

## USHER'S EXTRA

Blended and bottled by J. & G. Stewart Ltd, 9/13 Maritime Street, Leith, Edinburgh EH6 6SG. Andrew Usher owned Edinburgh Distillery, sold Glenlivets and was the first to start blending. He was one of the group that built the North British Distillery in 1887 in opposition to DCL. Stewarts were tea and wine merchants in the 18th century and incorporated Andrew Usher & Co. and James Gray & Sons, joining DCL in 1918. They operate Coleburn-Glenlivet Highland malt distillery. This is a good de luxe blend of grains and malts in the Usher tradition.

**Usher's Green Stripe**, the standard brand, is known for its charm and consistency.

**Usher's O.V.G.** (Old Vatted Glenlivet) is a pleasantly mature blend.

**Jamie Stuart** is a popular standard brand.

**Antique Jamie Stuart** is a mature de luxe brand from this old blending firm.

**Usher's Special Reserve** is a mature "Old Vatted Glenlivet," the kind of drink in which the pioneer blender specialised.

## VAT 69

Blended and bottled by Wm Sanderson & Sons, The Loan, South Queensferry, West Lothian. Ninety years ago William Sanderson, blending in a series of vats, got his friends together to choose the best. The concensus of opinion (and it was his own) was that the 69th vat was the best. The brand is world-renowned and very popular in West Germany. There are also **Vat 69 Gold** and **Vat 68.** Sandersons blend and bottle for other DCL labels, and distil at Hillside, Montrose.

## WATSON'S NO. 10

Blended and bottled by James Watson & Co. Ltd, Seagate, Dundee DD1 3EN, another DCL company. This is a sterling blend with a friendly warmth and gentility.

**Baxter's Barley Bree** is a cheery blend which has achieved great acceptance.

## WHITE HORSE

Blended and bottled by White Horse Distillers Ltd, 120 St Vincent Street, Glasgow G2 5HW. A popular blend with a long history and an international reputation.

James Logan Mackie & Co., grocers, were associated with Captain Graham in the development of Lagavulin Islay malt distillery and "White Horse" began as a blend based on the product with grain whisky employed to modify the peat-reek Islay malt flavour. The name was taken from White Horse Inn at the foot of the Canongate near Holyrood Palace, Edinburgh, and close to family properties of the Mackies. Sir Peter Mackie ("Restless Peter") pioneered in the world marketing of Scotch. In 1924

*Above*
One of the famous Speyside distilleries—the Imperial, at Carron, which produces malt whisky for the DCL.

*Right*
At DCL Burghead Maltings in Morayshire the annual output is 50,000 tons. The green malt is seen being discharged for drying on a kiln floor, where it is flavoured by the application of peat smoke, an essential stage in the production of Highland malt whisky.

## TESTING . . .

Blending is the art of combining a large number of "single" whiskies from individual distilleries so that each makes its contribution to the blend. Robert Bookless, White Horse production director testing samples of single whiskies, which is always done by "nosing," never by drinking.

## AND TASTING

The author (*centre*) enjoys a glass with a friend in George Robertson's 37 Bar, famous even in Edinburgh's Rose Street for its vast selection of blends and fine old malts.

Mackie & Co. became White Horse Distillers Ltd. They were the first to use the screw cap as a handier method of sealing whisky bottles. Where "White Horse" (its name suggests purity and strength) is blended and bottled in Glasgow, there are headquarters with a computer service. About 40 whiskies go into the blends there are more than 50 different types of bottles and more than 700 variations of the label to suit the far-flung markets, for, as they say, "You can take a White Horse anywhere."

**Laird o' Logan.** A de luxe brand from White Horse Distillers Ltd.

**Logan's de Luxe.** A high class blend for the choosy drinker.

**White Horse Liqueur.** A grand after-dinner drink.

## WHYTE & MACKAY'S SPECIAL

Blended and bottled by Whyte & Mackay, 50 Wellington Street, Glasgow C.2 (offices also at 62 Pall Mall, London, S.W.1). James Whyte and Charles Mackay combined in 1882 and introduced this light-flavoured whisky made of 30 different malts. In 1960 they amalgamated with McKenzie Bros of Dalmore. Associated with Sir Hugh Fraser, Bt. (Scottish & Universal Investments Ltd). Major Hartley Whyte described his family's Special as "most subtly blended," and it is one of the most popular brands. There are also **W. & M. Supreme,** heavier, more malty, and **W. & M. 21 years old,** "every drop matured in oak casks for not less than 21 years," a very special drink indeed.

## YE AULD TOUN

Blended and bottled by John Gillon & Co. Ltd, 5 Oswald Street, Glasgow, the distillers of Glenury-Royal Highland malt whisky at Stonehaven, Kincardineshire. Theirs is a likeable de luxe blend of mature grains and vatted old malts with a full flavour and a pleasant after-taste.

**King William IV V.O.P.** is another distinctive and palatable brand from these DCL distillers and blenders.

## YELLOW LABEL

Blended and bottled by John Robertson & Son Ltd, 10 Links Place, Leith, Edinburgh EH6 7HA. This is an established Leith blending firm incorporated in DCL, and the blend has won a steady place with its strength, maturity and smoothness.

## YE WHISKY OF YE MONKS

Blended and bottled by yet another DCL subsidiary, Donald Fisher Ltd, 12 Howden Street, Edinburgh EH8 9HL. A de luxe blend of mature grains and a variety of Scotch malts.

**Ye Monks** and **Dew of Ben Lawers** are standard blends from this firm, and both are popular for their maturity, flavour and smoothness.

# 8 Scotch Around the World

SCOTLAND MAKES well over a hundred million proof gallons of Scotch whisky every year, about 50 million of malt whisky and 70 million of grain whisky. The total production of potable spirit warehoused or exported in 1972 was 167,638,000 proof gallons. At the end of 1971 there were 852,200,000 proof gallons of whisky in bonded warehouses in Great Britain.

Where does all that whisky go? Scotch forms a substantial part of the 12 million gallons of spirit for home use. Over 100,000 gallons to the Channel Islands, over 800,000 delivered as ship and aircraft stores or supplied to duty-free shops, about 70 million proof gallons exported to the value of over £200 million. Seventeen million proof gallons to the European Economic Community and other markets on that Continent, over 40 million proof gallons to the Americas (30 million to the U.S.A., the biggest overseas market for Scotch).

Almost two million to Australia and half a million to New Zealand and other parts of Australasia. Over four and a half million to Asia, including well over two million to Japan. About

111

a million to South Africa and a million and a half to other parts of Africa.

Our leading customers for Scotch are U.S.A., France, Western Germany, Italy, Japan, Australia, Canada, Belgium, Brazil and Venezuela, in that order. The largest exports of our malt whisky in bulk are to Japan and Brazil, both over the million mark.

In a list of nations taking Scotch whisky in 1971 and 1972 the only blanks are Albania, Bhutan, Faroe Islands, Macao, Mongolia, North Vietnam. China imports about a million proof gallons to the value of about £4 million, the Soviet Union about 50,000 proof gallons at a value of £180,000, and other Iron Curtain countries are substantially represented.

White Horse Distillers Ltd say: "You can get White Horse today in Mongolia, in Alaska, in the wilds of Africa. It is *the* drink in France."

John Haig & Co. Ltd say: "The name of Haig is the same, or nearly the same, in every language. It has become a fashionable international drink equally in place at a business convention in America or a chic wedding in Paris."

Long John Distilleries Ltd put it this way: "There are few countries in the world wherein you will fail to find at least one of our whiskies—Laphroaig, Black Bottle, Long John, Long John de Luxe, Islay Mist or Tormore. Countries to avoid, for the time being, include North Korea, the Yemen, Mongolia and Mahli. Elsewhere, you can generally ask for your Scotch by name: make sure that you get it!"

Even such countries as have some good whiskies of their own— Ireland, the United States, Canada, Australia and Japan—acknowledge that they have nothing like Scotch, and that Scotch can be made only in Scotland.

In the States, Scotch exporters have their own offices and also a network of distributors, each with his own territory. Hence the multiplicity of labels for the export market. But the names of the famous brands are the same.

"Harrods" is to be sold in the United States by an important company, and in Japan it will be imported by the Sony Trading Corporation and distributed through the Mitsukoshi Department Store Group, which enjoys in that country the kind of prestige which Harrods enjoys in Britain. Arrangements for the marketing of "Harrods" de luxe in other countries abroad are in progress.

Some of the malts I have mentioned already are popular abroad—Aberlour, Glenburgie, "Glen Ila" from Caol Ila (Islay), and a special one for export,"Justerini & Brooks 20 years old Finest Malt."

Among the 170 nations drinking Scotch, with U.S.A. in the lead, such a brand as "Cutty Sark" (Berry Bros & Rudd Ltd) is universal. The Scotch most in demand in the States is "J. & B. Rare" (International Distillers and Vintners). Two others making their mark are "Catto's Rare Highland" and "Old Mathew." "Cluny" (from Mackinlay-McPherson of Leith) is popular particularly in California, and is now advancing in the European market.

"Queen Anne" (Hill, Thomsons) sells well in Europe, the Far East, the Middle East and South Africa. "Johnnie Walker" is world famous. "Black & White" is another world beater. "Vat 69" (Wm Sanderson & Sons) has a commanding place in the Australian, South African, Canadian, Swedish and European Economic Community markets.

McCallum's "Perfection" is a favourite in the Antipodes. "Dewar's"—especially "White Label" but also "Dewar's Special" and "Ne Plus Ultra"—challenges "J. & B." in the American market.

De luxe brands made for export include "Ambassador Royal" (Hiram Walker—Taylor & Ferguson Ltd), "Angus McKay 8 year old" (Riverside), "Brae Dew" (McClelland), "Huntly De-Luxe" (Slater, Roger), Mackinlay's "Legacy" 12 years old, "Isle of Skye Old Liqueur Scotch Whisky" (Ian Macleod, Inverness), "J.G.T. de Luxe Reserve" (J. G. Thomson), "Long John 8 y.o." and "Long John 12 y.o." (Schenley), "Malcolm Stuart" (Melrose-Drover).

"Pinch" (John Haig & Co. Ltd), "Royal Ages" (Justerini & Brooks), "Royal Vat" (Arthur Bell & Sons), "Shaw's Rare Old, Light, Reserve" 8 years old (Thomas Shaw, London and Glasgow), "Spey Royal 8 Years Old" (International), "The Monarch" (Lambert Bros, Edinburgh), "William Lawson" (Clan Munro, Coatbridge).

The other export brands run into thousands. They include "Baird's" (Baird-Taylor Ltd), "Ben Cally" (DCL), "Clanroy" (McClelland), "Clan Stewart" (DCL), "Craig Castle" (White Horse), "Dandie Dinmont" (A. Alexander, Edinburgh), "Deerstalker" (J. G. Thomson, Glasgow), "Donald's" (Macnish), "Duncan's Reserve" (Campbell & Clark), "Dundee Cream of Scotch Reserve" (Morton), "Fedcal" (International), "Gillons 'G' Blended" (DCL).

"Glen Laggan" (Hiram Walker), "Gold Thimble" (Hiram Walker), "Grey Label" (DCL), "Highland Fling" (Hiram Walker), "Highland Rover" (Hiram Walker), "House of Lords" (White Horse), "Huntly Blend" (DCL).

"King Arthur" and "King Charles" (DCL), "King Edward I" (Clan Munro), "King's Favourite" (McClelland), "King's Legend" (DCL), "King's Pride" (McClelland).

"Loretto" (DCL), "Lowrie's Scotch Malt," "Mackie's Ancient Scotch" (White Horse), "Mackinnon's 86°," "Marlboro" (DCL), "Marshall's" (Hiram Walker).

"Mary Stuart" (Fraser Stuart, Glasgow), "Northern Scot" (Scottish & Newcastle), "Old Court" (A. Gillies, Glasgow), "Old Grantian" 12 years old and blended 86° proof (Old Grantian Co. Ltd, Glasgow), "Old Matured" (DCL), "Queen's Own" (Grants of St James Ltd), "Red, White & Blue" (White Horse), "Royal Lochnagar" special for Canada (John Begg Ltd).

"Royal Crag" (Macnish), "Royal Escort" (Gillies).

"St Dennis" (Macnish), "Sandy Thomson" (The Glenfyne Distillery Co. Ltd, Glasgow), "Scottish Cream" (The Kinloch Distillery Co. Ltd, Glasgow), "Special Export Reserve" (Geo. & J. G. Smith of The Glenlivet).

"Stewart's Dundee," (Stewart & Son of Dundee Ltd), "Stewart's Finest Old" (J. & G. Stewart Ltd—DCL), "Strath-Roye" and "Scottish Envoy" (Strath-Roye Blenders Ltd, London), "Strong's Scotch Whisky" (W. & S. Strong Ltd, Glasgow), "Swing" (John Walker & Sons, Kilmarnock—DCL), "Talisman" (Lambert Bros, Edinburgh), "Tam o' Shanter" (Lang Bros Ltd, Glasgow), "Taplows" (Taplows Ltd, Glasgow), "The Kilty" (J. G. Turney & Son Ltd, Glasgow), "The Real MacTavish" (Ainslie & Heilbron—DCL), "Thomsons" (J. G. Thomson, Glasgow), "Tranquility" (Campbell & Clark).

"Usher's Special Reserve," for Canada (J. & G. Stewart, Edinburgh—DCL).

"White Label" (John Dewar & Sons Ltd, Perth—DCL) achieved second place in the United States market, selling over two million cases there in 1971, more than a million cases in New York alone. In the States they pronounce it "Doo-ers."

"William Lawson 8 y.o." (Clan Munro Whisky Ltd, Coatbridge), "Windsor Castle" (R. H. Thomson & Co.—Distillers—Ltd, Leith).

# 9    How to Drink It

THERE IS a story of the late Duke of Windsor when he was King Edward VIII. It may be apocryphal, but I have heard it told by railwaymen. In the course of his brief and uncrowned reign, he came north to the Highlands in the Royal train and was shunted into a quiet siding for his overnight sleep. In the morning a deputation of railway high brass had arranged to pay a courtesy call and inquire if he was comfortable. It was assumed that the King would offer them a morning dram. It was assumed equally that it would be their duty to accept the libation. This greatly perturbed a staunch teetotaller of the party, who found himself divided in his loyalty— to his monarch or his principles.

When they eventually saw the King, sure enough there he was, in pyjamas and dressing gown, and with a bottle of good Scotch in his hand, ready to dispense regal hospitality. He filled a glass and handed it to the teetotaller. That worthy, deciding that he would get it down like castor oil, turned his eyes up to Heaven and contracted his nostrils and threw the lot down his gullet in one draught.

The King looked at him admiringly and said: "What a man! Have another!"

True or no, it illustrates how not to drink Scotch. There may be those dangerous moments when the individual declares: "I need a stiff drink," and is concerned only to hit the stomach—at great risk to the liver—hard and quickly. That is when Scotch, or any other potent spirit, can be a menace. "I need a drink" should be listed among famous last words. And it is unfair to a pleasant beverage which experts have toiled to distil, mature, blend and bottle, to toss it down as if it were rotgut or red-eye, castor oil or Gregory's mixture. It is a drink to be sipped, savoured and enjoyed.

Whisky is normally drunk out of a tumbler or a goblet. The shape of the glass does little to detract from or enhance the pleasure. There is perhaps aesthetic satisfaction and a sense of status in handling a well-cut crystal whisky tumbler.

Whisky goes well with most foodstuffs and does not sit ill, as has been alleged, with a diet of shellfish. Provided there is nothing wrong with the shellfish, and one is neither eating nor drinking carelessly, whisky goes well with oysters, mussels and other bivalves and molluscs. It is a good aperitif and may also be drunk throughout the meal. Officers of the Highland regiments pour it ritually on their haggis at Caledonian dinners and Burns suppers.

If one is tasting a single whisky, a de luxe or special blend, it is worth while to taste it neat before diluting. If you want to appreciate the bouquet before tasting it, you may use one technique of the blender—rub a little on the palms of your hands and cup your hands to your nose. A tulip glass may be used for sniffing purposes.

If your ambition is to drink like a connoisseur, I have listed the singles and de luxe brands which you might try. But there is nothing to be ashamed of in preferring a standard brand to a single or a de luxe, nor is there any reason to blush because you prefer it diluted to neat. At 70° proof or 75°—the usual strengths at which you will encounter it—Scotch may be drunk neat, but it can also stand the addition of water or ice. Fifty-fifty whisky and water leaves it still potent enough and does not kill its taste. Beyond that a Scot would say: "Dinna droun the miller!"

The best dilutant is Scottish water, especially from a Highland

116

spring. Mr Donald Mackinlay, the Leith blender associated with "Mackinlay's," "Legacy" and McPherson's "Cluny," also with the distilleries of Isle of Jura and Glenallachy, told me he liked to give his guests a dram at a mountain spring in the distillery countryside. "They always enjoy that." Ideally, whisky should be diluted with such water or from some lake such as Loch Katrine.

Other dilutants are a matter of taste. Scotch whisky drinkers frown most on lemonade, yet women are not the only ones to commit this sacrilege.

Sir Compton Mackenzie was shocked to find that his old Barra friend, the Coddy, imagined that lemonade improved the taste of whisky. I have seen old men in a pub in Caithness who obviously had the same idea. I trust they were not doing it to Neil Gunn's beloved Old Pulteney. In Lowland pubs a bottle of lemonade is left on the counter for whisky drinkers to help themselves, but it is a traumatic experience to find this in the best distillery country.

The popular stuff to put into whisky in the Lowlands at Hogmanay (New Year's Eve) is Crabbie's green ginger, itself an alcoholic beverage. Of the two kinds of non-alcoholic gingers, some prefer the dry and some the sweet. Again it is each to his own taste. No one has the right to dogmatise about what other people ought to drink.

A popular Scottish practice, particularly in the Industrial Belt, is to drink a nip or half of whisky followed by a half pint of beer, or a glass of Scotch followed by a pint of beer. Highlanders often drink their whisky neat and "chase" it with a glass of cold water.

There are whisky-based liqueurs and other concoctions, and even cocktails, with which I will deal in the next chapter. Whisky goes with most things, and is unlikely to spoil any of them. The other ingredients would be more likely to ruin your good whisky. However, here follow some harmless cocktails in which whisky plays an honourable part.

# 10 Liqueurs and Cocktails

FOREMOST AMONG whisky liqueurs in Scotland is Drambuie, the honeyed, herbal dram based on a secret formula held by the Mackinnon family since the fugitive Prince Charlie gave it to a captain of their Skye clan in gratitude for shelter in 1746. In 1906 Malcolm Mackinnon, proprietor of the old established whisky firm of W. Macbeth & Sons, decided to use the old family recipe for the manufacture of a liqueur for sale to the general public. It took him some years to break into the conservative Edwardian market, but his product caught on and when at length it was ordered for the cellars of the House of Lords it was well on its way to becoming world-renowned. Now it is the largest-selling liqueur in Britain and the only British liqueur exported to every open market in the world.

Drambuie (the name is from Gaelic, *dram buidheach*, "a drink that satisfies") is the ideal after-meal drink. It is also a tasteful ingredient for cooking and it is the base of quite a range of cocktails. Its American distributor is W. A. Taylor & Co., New York.

Ronald Morrison & Co. Ltd, Leith, relatively recently brought out another liqueur called "Glayva" (a phonetic spelling of the Gaelic *glé mhath*, "very good"). There are also "Highland Morn" and "Scotch Morn" (Joseph Hobson & Son Ltd, Leeds).

Atholl Brose Co. Ltd, associated with Atholl Brose (Exports) Ltd, produce a ready-made Atholl Brose. There are a Whisky Punch made by McRae Bros (Distillers) Ltd, Braeval, Aberfoyle, Scotland, and a "Scots Mac" whisky Mac made by J. Wham & Son (Largs) Ltd ("Wham's Dram," it is subtitled).

As for cocktails, there are many which may be made from whisky and quite a number from Drambuie. For some of the following I am indebted to John Haig & Co. Ltd, White Horse Distillers Ltd, the Scotch Whisky Association and the Drambuie Liqueur Co. Ltd. Some of the others are traditional Scotch whisky drinks:

ATHOLL BROSE. There are variants, some omitting the oatmeal, but most agree that heather honey (or nearest offer) is essential. Equal proportions of heather honey and fine oatmeal are mixed with water to a creamy consistency. A good helping of Scotch whisky is added. The mixture is stirred until frothy, bottled and laid away for a couple of days before serving, if you have such strength of will. I have had it instantly mixed by a barman from an Argyll and Sutherland Highlanders mess, and it was perfect. The official Murrays of Blair Atholl recipe recommended that the meal should be mixed with cold water to a thick paste and then strained. Of the creamy liquor resulting take four sherry glassfuls of it to four dessertspoonfuls of honey, and enough whisky to bring the mixture up to a quart. To be well shaken before being taken.

AYRSHIRE RELISH. A glass of whisky in a half pint of fresh milk, preferably from an Ayrshire herd. Serve chilled.

BLOOD AND SAND. Equal parts Scotch Whisky, Cherry Heering and orange juice.

BIRSE TEA. To a cup of good tea, well strained, add sugar and milk to taste and pour in a glass of Scotch whisky. A little grated nutmeg may be sprinkled on top of the cup.

CLAUDE McKAY. One glass Scotch. One glass Jamaica rum. Fill up with Ross's lime juice and a cube of ice.

119

**DERBY FIZZ.** Five dashes of lemon juice, one teaspoonful powdered sugar, one egg, three dashes of Curacao, one glass of Scotch. Beat up and fill the tumbler with soda water.

**EARTHQUAKE.** Equal parts gin, Scotch whisky and absinthe. (Absinthe makes the heart grow fonder.)

**FLYING SCOTSMAN.** Two and a half glasses Italian Vermouth. Three glasses Scotch. One tablespoonful of bitters and one tablespoonful of sugar syrup.

**HET PINT** (the traditional Edinburgh Hogmanay—New Year's Eve—drink, formerly served to passers-by by hospitable gentlemen with hot kettles full of the stuff). Bring a quart of Scotch pale ale to the boil. Beat up the white of an egg in two glasses of Scotch whisky, using a small quantity of ale in the beating. Pour the egg and whisky into the hot ale and bring back to the boil, adding cloves, cinnamon, nutmeg or spice to taste. Serve piping hot.

**HIGHLAND COFFEE.** Scotch, coffee, sugar and cream to taste.

**HIGHLAND COOLER.** One teaspoonful powdered sugar, the juice of half a lemon, two dashes of Angostura, one glass of Scotch and a cube of ice. Fill up with ginger ale.

**HIGHLAND SPECIAL.** Three glasses of Scotch, two glasses of French Vermouth, half a glass of orange juice. Mix and add a little grated nutmeg.

**HOGMANANNIE** (New Year's Morning). Separate the yolks from the whites of two eggs. Beat up the yolks with sugar and cream. Whip the white separately. Pour two large glasses of Scotch into the beaten yolks, add the whipped whites and stir before serving.

**LSD** (lemon, Scotch and Drambuie). Equal parts Drambuie, Scotch whisky and lemon juice.

**MAIRI BHAN** (pronounced *Mah-ree Vahn*). To one glass of Scotch add half a glass of fresh cream. Sip slowly.

**MARK TWAIN.** A large Scotch whisky in a tumbler, with the juice of a lemon, a tablespoonful of crushed sugar, and a dash of Angostura bitters. Fill up with iced water.

PRIZE COO. One glass Scotch in a pint of hot milk, sweetened with a teaspoonful of heather honey.

ROB ROY. Equal parts Scotch whisky and Italian Vermouth, with a dash of Angostura.

RUSTY NAIL. Equal parts Scotch Whisky and Drambuie.

SABBATH MORN. One glass of Scotch whisky in a glass of fresh cream. Add one tablespoonful of heather honey and stir vigorously.

SCOTCH CORDIAL (the Victorians made this in July). Put into a large jug a pound of ripe white currants stripped of their stalks. Add a quarter of an ounce of grated ginger, the rind of two lemons and a quart of whisky. Let the mixture remain for 24 hours closely covered in the jug. Strain through a hair sieve, add one pound of lump sugar, and let it stand twelve hours longer, then bottle and cork it well. (People were patient in those days.)

SCOTCH HORSE'S NECK. Lemon juice, Scotch whisky and Angostura. Fill up with ginger ale.

SCOTCH RICKEY. One lump of ice, the juice of half a lime, the juice of quarter of a lemon, one glass of Scotch. Fill up with soda water.

STONE FENCE. Two ounces Scotch Whisky in a long tumbler with a cube of ice. Fill up with cider.

SUMMER SCOTCH. One glass of Scotch, three dashes of creme de menthe, one lump of ice. Fill tumbler up with soda.

SUSPENSION. Equal parts Crabbie's Green Ginger wine, Scotch whisky and orange squash. Mix well with ice and serve cold with a cherry.

THE GASLIGHT. One and a half ounces Scotch whisky, half an ounce Italian Vermouth and a dash of Angostura bitters. Pour in a thimbleful of Drambuie.

TODDY. Into a half pint tumbler pour a generous measure of Scotch whisky. Add an appropriate quantity of boiling water and a spoonful of sugar. Stir well. Add a slice of lemon and a spoonful of honey.

WHISKY MAC. Two thirds Scotch Whisky, one third Crabbie's Green Ginger wine. Some recipes recommend equal parts whisky and Green Ginger.

WHISKY PUNCH. Two glasses Scotch whisky. The juice of a lemon. A tablespoonful of sugar. Fill up with iced water and serve with slices of orange.

WHISKY SOUR. Double Scotch Whisky. Juice of half a lemon. Half a teaspoonful sugar. White of an egg. Shake with ice and serve with a squirt of soda.

WHISPER. Equal proportions of Scotch whisky, French Vermouth and Italian Vermouth. Serve in cracked ice.
Here are some Drambuie cocktails, in addition to LSD and The Gaslight already given:

ECSTASY. Equal parts Drambuie, cognac and French Vermouth. Serve with twist of orange peel.

FLORA MACDONALD. Quarter Drambuie, quarter dry gin, half French Vermouth.

GILDA. Quarter Drambuie, half gin, one eighth Lillet, one eighth Akvavit. Put cherry in glass and top with twist of orange peel.

ISLE OF SKYE. Equal parts Drambuie, gin and lemon juice.

MacKINNON. Four parts of Drambuie, one part Bacardi rum, two parts lemon juice and one part lime juice. Shake well. Serve in tall glasses with plenty of ice. Top with soda.

NORTH POLE COCKTAIL. Two-sixths Drambuie, one-sixth Bitter Campari Aperitivo, three-sixths vodka. (A KLM recipe.)

**PIONEER.** Equal parts Drambuie, Vodka de Kuyper, Orange Curacao Cusinier.

**POUSSE-CAFE.** Equal parts Creme de Cacao, Drambuie and cognac. Pour carefully into glass in that order so that ingredients float one on top of another.

**PRINCE CHARLIE.** Equal parts Drambuie, cognac and lemon juice.

**SHETLAND PONY.** Two parts Drambuie, three parts vodka, dash of lemon juice.

Lastly Mackie's own, a Scotch Breakfast. A bottle of whisky, a haggis and a collie dog. The dog is there to eat the haggis!

# Bibliography

Sir Robert Bruce Lockhart. *Scotch: the Whisky of Scotland in Fact and Story.* Putnam, 1959, and later editions.

R. J. S. McDowall. *The Whiskies of Scotland.* John Murray, 1967, and later editions.

David Daiches. *Scotch Whisky: its Past and Present.* André Deutsch, 1969.

James Ross. *Whisky.* Routledge & Kegan Paul, 1970.

Alfred Barnard. *The Whisky Distilleries of the United Kingdom.* Reprinted by David & Charles, 1969, from the original edition of 1887.

Ross Wilson. *Scotch: The Formative Years.* Constable, 1970.

John Wilson. *Scotland's Malt Whiskies.* Famedram Publishers, 1973.